Beyond the Closet Door!

Praise, Prayer, Practice and
Power of the Kingdom

GrannyE

WESTBOW
PRESS®
A DIVISION OF THOMAS NELSON
& ZONDERVAN

WestBow Press books may be ordered through booksellers or by contacting:

WestBow Press
A Division of Thomas Nelson & Zondervan
1663 Liberty Drive
Bloomington, IN 47403
www.westbowpress.com
844-714-3454

Scripture quotations marked AMP are taken from the Amplified® Bible, Copyright © 1954, 1958, 1962, 1964, 1965, 1987 by The Lockman Foundation. Used by permission

Scripture quotations marked NIRV are taken from the Holy Bible, NEW INTERNATIONAL READER'S VERSION®.Copyright © 1996, 1998 Biblica. All rights reserved throughout the world. Used by permission of Biblica.

Scripture marked NIV are taken from the Holy Bible, New International Version®. NIV®. Copyright © 1973, 1978, 1984 by International Bible Society. Used by permission of Zondervan. All rights reserved.

Scripture marked KJV are taken from the Holy Bible, King James Version (Authorized Version). First published in 1611. Quoted from the KJV Classic Reference Bible, Copyright © 1983 by The Zondervan Corporation.

ISBN: 978-1-6642-9239-0 (sc)
ISBN: 978-1-6642-9238-3 (e)

Print information available on the last page.

WestBow Press rev. date: 05/01/2023

Contents

Foreword

Now is the time – the set time for me to write this book. It has taken more than 30 years for the words of this book to come that God wanted me to put down on these pages.

When I was young in the Lord, the name Rudyard Kipling, would come to mind. He was an author who wrote several books. He was an author who uses simplicity in his writing so that anyone can read his books and understand. His themes, goals and desire were clearly conveyed to the reader from the pages of his books.

For years I expected to write a book, but I had no idea of a title or what the subject of the book would be. (**Psalm 39:3** – *"My heart was hot within me, while I was musing the fire burned: then spake I with my tongue."*) My desire for you the reader is that you will receive the principles, commands, love, wisdom and spiritual understanding from God and Holy Spirit.

Matthew 6:33 – *"But seek ye first the kingdom of God, and his righteousness, and all these things shall be added unto you."* This scripture is used throughout these pages that will permeate and become theme and main purpose to you receiving God's will for your life. It is time to <u>seek the</u> <u>Lord</u> and His Kingdom as never before. We need to do what God tells us to do in that scripture. It is exciting to seek (*look for with all your heart*) the kingdom and His righteousness (His way of doing and being right) and then all these things taken together will be given you besides. (Amp)

Our victory comes by going through the Door (Jesus is the Door). The Door that opens into the throne room of God. We have received through Jesus Christ (the Door) as the access into the throne room to seek God's help in times of need for ourselves and for others who are in needs of an answer.

Psalms 39:7 – "And now, Lord, what do I wait for and expect? My <u>hope</u> and <u>expectations</u> are in You."

We must be seekers of God's love for us through faith in Jesus Christ.

All scriptures are taken from the Amplified Bible unless otherwise, stated.

To Witness by Faith in the Word of God
(Luke 1:67-80; Isaiah 40:3, 9)

Now is the time, the set time, to be witnesses as they were in the 2nd verse of Luke 1, *they were eyewitnesses and ministers of the Word* (that is, of the doctrine concerning the attainment, through Christ of salvations in the Kingdom of God (Amp). Luke said his purpose was that the most excellent Theophilus may know the full truth and understand with certainty and security against error the accounts (histories) and doctrines of the faith of which you have been "orally" instructed (**v.4**).

My desire and purpose are to inform and instruct in my own simple way the same thing for the same reason. That certainty and security against error will not hinder us from the accounts (histories) which I translate as (His stories) H I S T O R I E S. A voice of one who cries: Prepare the wilderness (we all go through or are in the wilderness) the way of the Lord (clear away the obstacles), make straight and smooth in the desert a highway for our God (**Isa 40:3**)

And the glory (Majesty and splendor) of the Lord shall be revealed and all flesh shall see it together; for the mouth of the Lord has spoken it.

(Isaiah 40:5)

Proclaim, "The grass withers, the flower fades, but the word of our God will stand forever. (**Isaiah 40:8**)

Behold your God! (**Isaiah 40:9**) **Acts 10:36-43**

This is the contents of the message announcing the Good News (Gospel) of peace by Jesus Christ, who is Lord of all.

Now may the Lord of Peace, Himself grant you His Peace (the peace of His kingdom) at all times and in all ways (under all circumstances and conditions, whatever comes) the Lord be with you all. (**Second Thessalonians 3:16**).

My Edict: My Order or Decree

(Official Authoritative Regulation or Instruction to Announce Publicly with Conviction)

Isaiah 12: 1-6

1. *And in that day, you will say I will give thanks to You. O' Lord for though You were angry with me, Your anger has turned away and You comfort me.*

2. *Behold, God my salvation! I will trust and not be afraid, for the Lord God is my strength and song: Yes, He has become my salvation (deliverance, trust, redeemer)*

3. *Therefore, with joy will you draw water from the Wells of Salvation.*

4. *And in that day, you will say, Give thanks to the Lord, call upon His Name and by means of His Name (in solemn entreaty); <u>declare and make known His deeds among the peoples of the earth, proclaim that his Name is exalted!</u>*

5. *Sing praises to the Lord for He has done excellent things (gloriously); <u>let this be made known to all the earth.</u>*

6. *Cry aloud and shout joyfully, you <u>women</u> and <u>inhabitants</u> of Zion (church) for great in your midst is the Holy One of Israel.*

7. *For your (my) eyes have seen all the great work of the Lord which he did.*

Deuteronomy 11:1

1. *Therefore, you shall love the Lord your God and keep His charge (task or responsibility, command) His statutes (laws) His precepts (rules or action or conduct) and His commandments (orders) always.*

The Seed of the Word of God

(The Secret Power of the Kingdom)
Ephesian 3:20 Amp

Dare 2 Believe – We dare to have the boldness of free access (an undeserved approval to God) – **Ephesians 3:12**

Isaiah 2:8: *Ask of Me, and I will give You the nations as Your inheritance and the uttermost parts of the earth as your possession* Praise, Prayer, Practice and Power of the Kingdom.

Esther 4:14: And who knows but that you have come to the kingdom, for such a time as this and for this very occasion.

Matthew 25:31: When the Son of Man comes in His Glory His Majesty and Splendor and all the holy angels with Him. Then He will sit on the throne of His Glory.

Matthew 25:32: All nations will be gathered before Him, and He will separate them (the people) from one another as a shepherd separated his sheep from the goats.

Matthew 25:33-34: And He will cause the sheep to stand at His right hand but the goats at His left. Then the king will say to those at His right hand. Come, you blessed of My father (you are favored of God and appointed to eternal salvation), inherit (receive as your own) the kingdom prepared for you from the foundations of the world.

John 3:3*:* Jesus answered him, I assure you, most solemnly I tell you, that unless a person is <u>born again</u> (anew, from above) he cannot ever see (know, be acquainted with, and experience) the kingdom of God.

John 3:5*:* Jesus answered, I assure you most solemnly, I tell you, unless a man is born of water and (even) the Spirit, he cannot (ever) enter the Kingdom of God.

Galatians 4:31: So, brethren we (who are born again) are not children of a slave woman (the natural) but of the free (the supernatural.)

Calvary (song)

1. Years I spent in vanity and pride caring not my Lord was crucified, knowing not it was for me, He died. On Calvary!

2. By God's word at last my sin I learned, then I trembled at the Law I'd spurned, till my guilty soul imploring turned to Calvary.

3. Now I've given to Jesus everything now I gladly own Him as my King Now my raptured soul can only sing of Calvary.

4. O the love that drew salvation's plan! O the grace that brought it down to man! O the mighty gulf that God did span at Calvary

Chorus

Mercy there was great, and grace was free. Pardon, there was multiplied to me, There my burdened soul found liberty, at Calvary!

Ephesians 3:12: In whom, because of our faith in Him, we dare to have the boldness (courage and confidence) of free access (an unreserved approach to God with freedom with our fear.)

Ephesian 3:20-21: Now to Him Who by (in consequence of) (the action of His power that is at work within us), is able to (carry out His Purpose) and do superabundantly far over and above all that we (dare) ask or think (infinitely beyond our highest prayers, desires, thoughts, hopes or dreams). To Him be glory in the church and in Christ Jesus throughout all generations forever and ever. Amen (So be it).

Acquaintance and Dedication, Consecration And Declaration in Your Prayer

(Praise to God, Prayer to God, Practice – do act upon, carry out, Power in the Holy Spirit)

Hebrew 10:14: For by a single offering, He has forever completely cleansed and perfected those who are consecrated made holy.

Job 22:21-26: I acquaint, now myself with Him (God the Father, God the Son, God the Holy Spirit) and I agree with God and show yourself/myself to be conformed to His Will, and be at peace, by that (you shall prosper and great) good shall come to me. *V.22.* As I pray, I receive the law and instruction from His mouth and lay up His words in your/my heart (*Psalms 119:11*). *v.23* As I return to the Almighty (and submit and humble myself before Him)., I will be built up; if I put away unrighteousness for from my tents (dwelling places). *V.24* As I lay gold in the dust and the gold of Ophir among the stones of the brook (considering them of little worth). *V.25* And as I make the almighty my gold and the Lord my precious silver treasures, *v.26* Then I have delight in the Almighty and I life up my face to God, I make my <u>prayer</u> to Him, and He will hear me, and I will pay my vows.

Philippians 1:9-11 – I pray that my love may abound yet more and more and extend to its <u>fullest development</u> in <u>knowledge</u> and all keen insight that my love may display itself in greater depth of <u>acquaintance</u> and more <u>comprehensive discernment</u>. So that I may surely learn to sense what is vital and approve and prize what is excellent and of real value (recognizing the highest and the best, and distinguishing the moral differences), and that you may be untainted and unerring and blameless (so that with hearts sincere and certain and unsullied, I may approach the day of Christ (not stumbling nor causing others to stumble.) May I abound in and be filled with the fruits of righteousness (of right standing with God and right doing) which comes through Jesus Christ.

Hosea 6:3: Yes, let us know (recognize, be acquainted, with, and understand) Him: let us be zealous to know the Lord (to appreciate, give heed to, and cherish Him). His going forth is prepared and certain as the dawn, and He will come to us as the (heavy) rain, as the latter rain that waters the earth.

John 4:10: Jesus answered her. If you had only known and had recognized God's gift and who this is that is saying to you, Give me a drink, you would have asked Him (instead) and He would have given you living water.

John 4:42: And they told the woman, Now we no longer believe (trust, have faith) just because of what you said; for we have heard Him ourselves (personally), and we know that He truly is the Savior of the world, the Christ.

First Peter 2:5: (Come) and like living stones, be yourselves built (into) a spiritual house for a holy (dedicated, consecrated) priesthood, to offer up (those) spiritual sacrifices (that are) acceptable and pleasing to God through Jesus Christ.

First *Peter 2:9:* But you are a chosen race, a royal priesthood, a dedicated nation (God's) own purchased special people that you may set forth the wonderful deeds and display the virtues and perfections of Him Who called you out of darkness into His marvelous light.

The King and His Kingdom
(Prayer, Praise, Practice, and Power in the Kingdom)

The Zeal of the Lord of host will perform this. **Isaiah 9:6-7 (Amp)**

Daniel 2:44: And in the days of these (final ten) kings shall the God of Heaven set up a kingdom which shall never be destroyed, nor shall its sovereignty be left to another people, but it shall break and crush and consume all these kingdoms and it shall stand forever.

Daniel 7:14: And there was given Him (the Messiah) dominion and glory and kingdom, that all peoples, nations, and languages should serve Him. His dominion is an everlasting dominion which shall not pass away, and <u>His</u> kingdom is one which shall not be destroyed.

Daniel 7:18: But the saints of the Most High (God) shall receive the kingdom and possess the kingdom forever, even forever and ever.

Daniel 7:22: Until the Ancient of Days came, and judgement was given to the saints of the Most High (God) and the time came when the Saints possessed the kingdom

Luke 19:38: Saying, Blessed by the King that cometh in the Name of the Lord; peace in Heaven, and glory in the highest. Blessed be He that cometh in the Name of the Lord. (**Psalms 118:26**)

Acquaintance and Dedication, Consecration and Dedication in Your Prayer Time

Philippians 1:11: (The Anointed One), to the honor and praise of God (that His glory may be both manifested and recognized).

I shall also decide and decree a thing and it shall be established for (me) and the light (of God's favor) shall shine upon my ways. When they make me low, I will say, There is a lifting up; and the humble person He lifts up and saves. He will even deliver the one (for whom I intercede) who is not innocent; yes, He will be delivered through the cleanness of my hands. (**Job 42:7-8** reference of Job intercession for his friends) How precious and weighty also are Your thoughts to me, O God! How vast is the sum of them. (My thoughts how God still loves me!) He knows me and yet he loves me. How wonderful is that to me! Hallelujah! Hallelujah! (**Psalms 139:1-17)**

Psalm 40:16: I love your salvation and I will say continually, The Lord be magnified;

Jeremiah 29:11: *(As for me) I am poor and needy, yet the Lord takes thoughts and plans for me, You are my Help and my Deliverer. O my God do not tarry!* **(Psalms 70:1-5** and **First Peter 5:7)**

Jeremiah 24:7: And I will give them a heart to know (recognize, understand, and be acquainted with Me), (Father God) that I am the Lord; and they will be My people; And I will be their God for they will return to Me with their whole heart. In the Name of Jesus; Amen and Amen.

Hebrew 8:11: And it will nevermore be necessary for each one to teach his neighbor and his fellow-citizen or each one his brother, saying, know (perceive, have knowledge of, and get acquainted by experiences with the Lord, for all will know Me, from the smallest to the greatest of them.

Job 19:25: For I know that the Redeemer and Vindicator lives, and at last He (the Last One) will stand upon the earth.

Isaiah 44:6: *Thus says the Lord, the KING of Israel and His Redeemer, the Lord of hosts: I am the First and I am the Last; besides Me there is no Go,* (**Revelation 1:17,2:8,22:13**)

Isaiah 44:7: Who is like Me? Let him (stand and) <u>proclaim</u> it, <u>declare</u> it, and set (his proofs) in order before Me. Since I made and established the people of antiquity. (Who has announced, from of old) the things that are coming? Then let them <u>declare</u> the future things. **v.8:** Fear not; nor be afraid (in the coming violent upheavals); have I not told it to you from of old and <u>declared it</u>? And you are My witnesses! Is there a God besides Me? There is no (other) Rock! I know not any.

Isaiah 41:4: Who has prepared and done this, calling forth and guiding the destinies of the generation (of the nations) from the beginning? I, the Lord – the first (existing before <u>his-tory</u> began) and with the last (an ever present, unchanging God) – I Am He.

The King and His Kingdom Prophecy

Daniel 2:44; First Corinthians 15:23-28 and Hebrew 1:8-9

Isaiah 9:6-7 (NIRV): A child will be born to us, A son will be given to us, He will rule over us, and He will be called <u>Wonderful</u>, <u>Adviser</u>, and <u>Mighty God</u>. He will also be called <u>Father Who Lives Forever</u> and <u>Prince Who Brings Peace</u>. The authority of His rule will continue to grow.

The peace He brings will never end. He will rule on David's throne and over His Kingdom. He will make the Kingdom strong and secure. His rule will be based on what is fair and right. It will last forever.

The Lord's great love will make sure that happens. He rules over all.

Isaiah 9:6-7 (Amp): For to us a Child is born, to us a Son is given, and the government shall be upon His Shoulders, and His Name shall be called <u>Wonderful</u>, <u>Counselor</u>, <u>Mighty God</u>, <u>Everlasting Father (of Eternity)</u>, <u>Prince of Peace</u>, of the increase of His government and of peace there shall be no end, upon the throne of David and over His Kingdom to establish it and to uphold it with justice and with righteousness from the (latter) time forth, even forevermore. The zeal of the Lord of host will perform this.

NIRV: New International Revised Version

Fruit of the Spirit, The Precious Word, God's Presence

1. Advancement of the Kingdom – through service
2. Revelation of the Kingdom – through prayer
3. Expanding the Kingdom – through use

1. Advance – promote bring or move forward, improvement
2. Revelation – to make known profoundly, enlightening.
3. Expand – enlarge, to make bigger, use the resources that God has given is: Word of God in many translations. Word of mouth (witnessing). Television programs, other media programs. Missionaries: giving and sending into all the World and preaching the gospel of the kingdom. (**Colossians 4:2**)

Matthew 9:35: And Jesus went about all the cities and villages, teaching in their synagogues and proclaiming the good news (the Gospel of the kingdom and curing all kinds of diseases and every weakness and infirmity.

Psalm 45:1: My heart overflow with a goodly theme. I address my psalm to a King; my tongue is like the pen of a ready writer.

Psalm 45:6: Your throne, O God is forever and ever the scepter of righteousness is the scepter of your kingdom.

Lamentations 5:19: But You, O Lord remain and reign forever, Your throne endures from generation to (all) generations.

Hebrew 4:18: Let us then fearlessly and confidently and boldly draw near to the throne of grace (the throne of God's unmerited favor to us sinners) saved by His Grace that we may receive mercy (for our failures) and find grace to help in good times for every need (appropriate helps and well- timed help) coming when we need it.

My desire is that there will be something within these to inspire you (the reader) to seek God's Kingdom as never before. The good news of the Gospel of the Kingdom is so exciting because "we' are awaiting on Jesus.

Serving him and so He tells us to-be-about the Father's business. Live excited! Live in expectancy! Breathe God's precious air and enjoy every day – your life-your – eternal life and hope to the end. Occupy until I come, says the Lord!

First Corinthians 16:9: For a wide <u>door</u> of opportunity for <u>effectual</u> (service) has opened to me (there, a great and promising one) and (there are) many adversaries.

James 5:16 – 18: Confess your faults one to another and <u>pray</u> one for another that ye may be healed. The <u>effectual</u> fervent <u>prayer</u> of a righteous man availeth much. Elias was man subject to like passions as we are and he <u>prayed</u> earnestly that it might not rain, and it rained not on the earth by the space of three years and a month. And he prayed again, and the heavens gave rain and the earth brough forth her fruit.

As we keep knocking the Lord will certainly open the door and surely, He will answer our prayers.

Prayer, Praise, Power of Holy Spirit
Gospel of the Kingdom, the King, and His Kingdom

Zechariah 4:9: The Lord has sent me to you as His Messenger, Grace (Protection)

Psalm 12:6: The Words and intimate Promises of the Lord are pure Words, like silver refined in an earthen furnace, purified seven times over.

Proverbs 7:2: Keep my commandments and live and keep my law and teaching as the apple (the pupil of your eye).

Proverbs 7:3: Bind them on your fingers, write them on the tablet of your heart.

Proverbs 22:11: A word fitly spoken and in due season is like apples of gold in settings of silver.

The ethical and spiritual principles of the Messianic kingdom are emphasized indicating that the kingdom has a present spiritual existence as well as a future material manifestation.

Luke 17:21: Now the Kingdom of God is in us (the believer) <u>in our hearts</u> and <u>surrounding us.</u>

We have been given authority be God, we are to take authority; and to walk as Children of God. We are lights in the darkness, and we know that we are anointed to bring souls into the kingdom of God. We must walk in love to those on the outside of the kingdom, and always walk in love with your brothers and sisters in Christ.

Be a prayer warrior. Win some to Christ. Bring them into the <u>Kingdom of God,</u> snatch them from Satan, that old toothless snake, seeking whom he may devour. <u>Pray</u> and <u>testify</u> to the glory of God.

Matthew 28:20: Jesus said teach them to observe everything that I have commanded you and behold I (Jesus) am with you all the days to the very close and consummation of the ages. Amen (So let it be)

Make disciples (learners) for the kingdom. "On your knees; you can change situations, places, times, circumstances and people with your prayers." Your prayers are the way to join with the Father, Jesus and the Holy Spirit in changing the world around you. Through the Holy Spirit helping us in our prayer life we can do as they did in **Acts 12**.

When Herod killed James, John's brother and Herod saw how that pleased the Jews, he proceeded farther by arresting Peter at Passover week and put Peter in prison. While Peter was in prison, the church assembly made <u>fervent</u> and <u>persisten</u>t prayer to God was gong forth for his release.

Acts 12:6-7: The very night before Herod was about to bring him forth, Peter was sleeping between two soldiers fastened with two chains and sentries before the door were guarding the prison. And suddenly an angel of the Lord appeared (standing beside him) and a light shone in the place where he was and the angel gently smote Peter on the side and awakened him, saying, Get up quickly! And the chains fell off his hands.

What a change! The fervent and persistence in praying has brought about. It was so; that Peter thought he was seeing a vision. When he came to himself, he know that the Lord had sent an angel and delivered him from the hand of Herod and from what the others expected to do to him. He went to John-Mark's mother's house, there were a large number of people, assembled together <u>praying</u>, and they were amazed to see Peter out of prison. It will be amazing to see the answers to your prayers also. It's time to pray, pray, pray for people to some now into the Kingdom of God. "Release them now!"

James 5:19-20: Brethren, if anyone among you strays from the truth and falls into error and another person brings him back (to God). Let the (latter) one be sure that whoever turns a sinner from his evil course will save (that ones) soul from death and will cover a multitude of sins, (procure the pardon of the many sons committee by the convert.)

Second Timothy 2: 25-26: He must correct his opponents with courtesy and gentleness, in the hope that God may grant that they will repent and come to know the Truth (that they will perceive and recognize and become accurately acquainted with and acknowledge it). And that they may come to their senses (and) escape out of the snare of the devil having been held captive by him (henceforth) to do His (God's) will.

First Peter 4:2: (KJV) That, he no longer should live the rest of his time in the flesh to the lusts of men, but to the will of God

First Peter 4:17:(KJV) *For the time is come that judgment must begin at the house of God: and if it first begin at us, what shall the end be of them that obey not the gospel of God?* ***And if the*** ***righteous scarcely be saved, where shall the ungodly and the*** ***sinner appear****?*

First Peter 3:7 (KJV) *But the end of all things is at hand: be ye therefore sober and watch unto Prayer.*

Colossians 4:5-6: Behave yourselves wisely (living prudently and with discretion) in your relations with those of the outside world (the non-Christians). Making the very most of the time and seizing (buying up) the opportunity. Let your speech at all times be gracious (pleasant and winsome), seasoned (as it was) with salt, (so that you may never be at a loss) to know how you ought to answer anyone (who puts a question to you).

Colossians 4:11b: *...for the extension of God's kingdom*

Expanding the Kingdom Through Prayer and Witness

Reaching the Lost at any Cost

For God takes no pleasure in the death of the wicked:

Ezekiel 18:23 (KJV): Have I any pleasure at all that the wicked should die saith the Lord God! And not that he should return from his ways and live.?

Ezekiel 18:23 (AMP): Have I any pleasure in the death of the wicked? says the Lord, and not rather that he should turn from his evil way and return (to his God) and live?

v.27: Again, when the wicked man turns away from his wickedness which he has committed and does that which is lawful and right, he shall save his life.

v.32: For I have no pleasure in the death of him who dies, says the Lord God. Therefore turn (be converted) and live!

Second Peter 3:9: The Lord is not slack concerning his promise, as some men count slackness; but is longsuffering to usward not willing that any should perish, but that all should come to repentance.

Habakkuk 2:3: And the Lord answered, me and said; Write the vision, and make it plain upon tables that he may run that readeth it.

Proverbs 31:8: *Open your mouth for the dumb (those unable to speak for themselves) for the rights of all who are left desolate and defenseless* (**First Samuel 19:4; Esther 4:16; Job 29:15-16**).

Proverbs 31:9: *Open your mouth, judge righteously, and administer justice for the poor and needy.* (**Leviticus 9:15; Deuteronomy 1:16; Job 29:12; Isaiah 1:17; Jeremiah 22:16**)

Acts 8:12: But when they believed the good news (the Gospel) about the Kingdom of God and the Name of Jesus Christ (the Messiah) as Phillip preached it. They were baptized, both men and women.

Acts 12:5: So, Peter was kept in prison, but the fervent prayer for him was persistently made to God by the church (assembly).

Romans 1:16 For I am not ashamed of the Gospel (good news) of Christ, for it is God's power working unto salvation (for deliverance from eternal death) to everyone who believes with a personal trust and a confident surrender and firm reliance to the Jew first and also to the Greek (Gentiles).

First Corinthians 16:9: For a wide door of opportunity for effectual (service) has opened to me (there, a great and promising one), and there are) many adversaries.

Entrance into the Kingdom of God Through the New Birth and Through the Power of Prayer

Psalms 78:23: Yet He commanded the clouds above and opened the <u>doors</u> of heaven.

Psalms 119:130: Entrance and unfolding of Your Words give <u>light</u>; their unfolding gives understanding (discernment and comprehension to the simple

John 8:37: (Yes) I know that you are Abraham's offspring: yet you plan to kill Me because my Word has no entrance (makes no progress, does not find any place) in you.

John 10:1-3: Enter by the <u>door</u>. And I give them eternal life. Enter by the <u>door</u> into the sheepfold, The watchman opens the <u>door.</u>

v.7: Jesus said …, that I Myself am the <u>Door</u>.

v.9: I am the <u>Door</u>; anyone who enters in through Me will be saved (will live). He will come in and he will go out (freely) and will find pasture (food).

v.11: I am the Good Shepherd, The Good Shepherd risks and lays down His own life for the sheep.

The World is our mission field. We must "Go into all the World and preach the Gospel of God and our Christ (the Messiah) our soon coming King."

Open wide the <u>Door.</u> Present the King and His <u>Kingdom</u>. Enlarge the <u>Door</u> show forth His <u>Power</u>. To reach out to the world: through <u>Intercessory prayer</u>, media, books, etc. Be transparent and open to transmit the <u>light</u> of the Holy <u>Spirit</u> so that He can do the work within you.

Second Peter 1:11: For so an <u>entrance</u> shall be ministered unto you abundantly into the everlasting kingdom of our Lord and Savior, Jesus Christ. (**Revised Version)** For thus shall be richly supplied unto you the <u>entrance</u> into Christ Kingdom, the Eternal Kingdom.

Acts 14:22: **(KJV)** Confirming the souls of the disciples, and exhorting them to continue in the faith, and that we through much tribulation <u>enter</u> into the Kingdom of God.

Acts 14:22: Establishing and strengthening the souls and hearts of the disciples, urging and warning and encouraging them to stand firm in the faith, and (telling them) (that it is through many hardships and tribulation we must <u>enter</u> the kingdom of God.

Acts 14:22: (NIRV) There they helped the believers gain strength. They told them to remain true to what they had been taught "We must go through many hard times to <u>enter</u> God's kingdom".

Second Peter 1:10-11: Therefore, my brothers, be all the more eager to make your calling and election sure. For if you do these things, you will never fall and you will receive a rich welcome into the eternal Kingdom of our Lord and Savior Jesus Christ.

James 1:2-4: Consider it wholly joyful my brethren, whenever you are enveloped in or encounter trials of any sort or fall into various temptations (trials test). Be assured and understand that the trial and proving of your faith bring out endurance and steadfastness and patience.

But let endurance and steadfastness and patience have full play and do a thorough work, so that you may be (people) perfectly and fully developed (with no defects), lacking in nothing.

James 1:2-4: (NIV) Consider it pure joy, my brethren whenever you face trials of many kind, because you know their the testing of your faith develops perseverance. Perseverance must finish its work so that you may be mature and complete, not lacking anything.

Psalms 119:130: The <u>entrance</u> and unfolding of Your words give light; their unfolding gives understanding (discernment and comprehension) to the simple.

NIV: New International Version

Salvation Prayer
An Entrance into the Kingdom of God

First Timothy 1:12 – 17: (Paul Speaking) But I obtained mercy for the reason that in me, as the foremost (of sinners), Jesus Christ might show forth and display all His perfect longsuffering and patience for an example to (encourage), those who would therefore after believe on Him for (the gaining of) eternal life. Now to the King of eternity, incorruptible and immortal, invisible the only God, be honor and glory forever and ever (to the ages of ages), Amen (So be it).

Second Timothy 2:4: Help me! Holy Spirit, to wage a good warfare and that I hold fast to faith and to the revelation of Jesus Christ that You are revealing in me. Help me, to lean my entire human personality on (You) God in absolute trust and confidence and having a good (clear) conscience, I aim to satisfy and please the one who enlisted me.

First Timothy 2:1-2: First of all, then I admonish and urge that petitions, prayers, intercession, and thanksgivings be offered on behalf of all men. For kings and all who are in positions of authority or high responsibility, that (outwardly) we may pass a quiet and undisturbed life: (and inwardly) a peaceable one in all godliness and reverence and seriousness in every way.

First Timothy 2:3 –8: For such (praying) is good and right, and (it is) pleasing and acceptable to God our Savior. Who wishes all men to be saved and (increasingly) to perceive and recognize and discern and know precisely and correctly the (divine) Truth. For there (is only) one God, and (only) one Mediator between God and men, the man Jesus Christ. Who gave Himself as a ransom for all (people, a fact that was) attested to at the right and proper time. I (Paul) desire therefore that in every place men should pray, without anger or quarreling or resentment or doubt (for their minds), lifting up holy hands.

Acts 2:21: And it shall be that whoever shall call upon the Name of the Lord (invoking, adoring, and worshiping the Lord Christ) shall be saved.

First Thessalonian 5:17: _Pray without ceasing_

Revelations 5:8c: …And golden vials full of odours, which are the prayers of God's people (the saints)

Proverbs 15:8b: … _But the prayers of the upright is His delight._

Matthew 21:13, 22; Acts 6:4; James 5:15-16; Second Chronicle 7:15: _Now my eyes will be open and my ears attentive to prayer offered in this place._

Acts 13:3-5: Then after fasting and praying, they put their hands on them and sent them away. So then, being sent out by the Holy Spirit, they went down to Seleucia, and from (that port) they sailed away to Cyprus. When they arrived at Salamis, they preached the Word of God (concerning the attainment through Christ of salvation in the Kingdom of God) in the synagogues of the Jews. And they had John (Mark) as an attendant to assist them.

While ministering to the Lord – the Holy spirit sent them out to do the work of God. We must also minister to the Lord as well. As we pray and worship God - things will be revealed to us.

Acts 12:24: The Word of the Lord (concerning the attainment through Christ of Salvation in the Kingdom of God) continued to grow and spread.

Acts 10:4: And he, gazing intently at him, became frightened and said, What is it, Lord? And the angel said to him, Your prayers and your (generous) gifts to the poor have come up (as a sacrifice) to God and have been remembered by Him.

Your prayers and gifts to the poor are a memorial.

Solomon's Prayer of Dedication of the Temple: He said

Second Chronicles 6:14-15: O Lord, God of Israel, there is no God like You in heaven or on earth… You who keep Your Covenant of

Love with Your Servants who continue wholeheartedly in Your way. You have kept Your promise to Your Servant David, my father, with Your Mouth You have promised and with Your Hand You have fulfilled it – as it is today.

Second Chronicles 6:40-42: Now, my god, may your eyes be open and your ears, attentive to the prayers offered in this place. Now arise, O Lord God, and come to you resting place. You and the ark of your might. May Your Priest, O Lord, God, be clothed with salvation, may Your Saints rejoice in Your Goodness. O Lord God do not reject Your Anointed One. Remember the great love promised to David Your Servant.

God appeared and answered Solomon at night after the dedication, worship, consecration, offering, and he had succeeded in carrying out all he had in mind to do in the Temple of the Lord and in his own palace.

Power of Prayer in the Gospel of the Kingdom

Colossians 4:2–4: Be earnest and unwearied and steadfast in your <u>prayer</u> (life), being both alert and intent in (your praying) with thanksgiving. And at the same time <u>pray</u> for us also that God may open a <u>door</u> to us for the Word (the Gospel), to proclaim the mystery concerning Christ (the messiah) on account of which I am in prison. What I may <u>proclaim</u> it fully and make it clear (speak boldly and unfold that mystery); as is my duty.

Colossians 4:12: Epaphras who is one of yourselves, a servant of Christ Jesus, sends you greetings. (He is) always striving for you earnestly in His <u>Prayers</u>, (pleading) that you may (as persons of ripe character and clear conviction) stand firm and mature (in spiritual growth) convinced and fully assured in everything willed by God.

First Thessalonians 3:10: (And we) continue to <u>pray</u> especially and with most intense earnestness night and day that we may see you face to face and mend and make good whatever may be imperfect and lacking in your faith.

First Thessalonians 5:17: *Be unceasing in <u>prayer</u> (<u>praying</u> perseveringly):*

First Thessalonians 5:25: *Brethren <u>pray</u> us.*

First Timothy 4:4–5: For everything God has created is good and nothing is to be thrown away or refused if it is received with thanksgiving. For it is hallowed and consecrated by the Word of God and by <u>prayers</u>.

First Timothy 5:5: Now (a woman) who is a real widow and is left entirely alone and desolate has fixed her <u>hope</u> on God and perseveres in <u>supplications</u> and <u>prayers</u> night and day.

Second Thessalonians 3:1: Furthermore, Brethren, do pray for us that the Word of the Lord may speed on (spread rapidly and run its course) and be glorified (extolled) and triumph, even as (it has done) with you.

Hebrew 13:18-19; James 5;13-16; First Peter 5:7

Seek the Lord! The Entrance into the Kingdom

Matthew 6:9-13b: OUR FATHER, who is in heaven, hallowed (kept holy) be Your Name. Your Kingdom come; Your Will be done on earth as it is in haven. For Yours is the <u>kingdom</u> and the <u>power</u> and the <u>glory</u> forever. Amen

Matthew 6:6 (KJV): But when you pray enter into, thy <u>CLOSET</u> and when thou hast shut the <u>Door,</u> pray to thy <u>FATHER</u> which in <u>SECRET</u> and your <u>FATHER</u> which seeth in <u>SECRET</u> shall <u>REWARD</u> thee openly.

Matthew 6:33: But <u>seek </u>(aim at and strive after) first of all <u>HIS KINGDOM</u> and <u>HIS RIGHTEOUSNESS</u> (His way of doing and being right) and then all these things taken together will be given you besides.

Psalms 24:5: He shall receive <u>blessing</u> from the Lord and <u>righteousness</u> from the God of His salvation. This is the generation (description) of those who <u>seek Him</u> (who inquire of and for Him and of necessity require Him) who seek Your Face (O God of) Jacob.

Selah (pause, and think of that)

Psalm 42:1: As the hart pants and longs for the water brooks, so I pant and long for You.

John 7:37-38; First Thessalonians 1:9-10: *O' God my inner self thirst for God for the Living God, When shall I come and <u>behold</u> the Face of God?*

First Thessalonians 2:12: To live lives worthy of God. Who calls you into His own <u>Kingdom</u> and the glorious blessedness (into which true believers will enter after Christ returns).

Matthew 7:7-8: Keep on asking and it will be given you; Keep on <u>SEEKING</u> and you will find; Keep on knocking (reverently) and (the

Door) will be opened to you. For everyone who keep on asking receives; and he who keeps on seeking finds; and to him who keep on knocking (the door) will be opened.

Matthew 24:33: So also, when you see these signs all taken together, coming to pass, you may know of a surety that He is near, at the very doors.

Psalms 24:6: This is the generation (description) of those who SEEK HIM (who inquire of and for HIM and of necessity require HIM), who SEEK YOUR FACE. (O' God of Jacob.) Selah, (pause, and think o that! (**Psalms 42:1**)

Pray, Pray, Pray, the Good News

(Gospel of the Kingdom)
Matthew 6:9

Pray therefore like this: (My Insight)

Knowledge and Praise to my Abba Father (Daddy)

Our Father, Who is in Heaven, Hallowed (kept Holy) be Your Name. We are His Children, and we must know we have dual citizenship.

We are citizens of Heaven, and we are citizens of Earth. The Creator, God endowed us with power from on high – He sent His only Son who died for our sins and is now living to intercede and intervene for us every day. Thanks to Our Father for the Holy Spirit who comes to indwell the believer (**First Peter 1:1-4,12; Psalm 4:7**) Everlasting Father (**Isaiah 9:6**) the Lord (**Psalms 23:7**) My Shepherd.

Praise and Honor to my Father:

Hallowed be Your Name – Your name is to be kept holy above all else. This is a worship key. Worship the Lord in the beauty of holiness and in holy array. Give Him the glory that's due the Lord. Be exalted O' Lord above all the earth. Bring an offering and come before Him. Tremble and reverently fear before Him. Honor and Majesty are found in His presence. Ascribe to the Lord glory and strength. Sing praises to His Name. (**Isaiah 9:6; 25:1; 40:9-11**) Good shepherd (**Psalm 23:1**)

God's Kingdom and God's Will

<u>Your Kingdom Come</u> – Your Authority is on earth as it is in Heaven. The Kingdom of God is preached, and it is attained by the believers of Christ, (the Messiah). As Jesus received authority on earth; through Him we receive that same authority because of the Gospel of the Kingdom. The Kingdom of God is within the believer in the believer's heart and among you, (surrounding you). (**Luke 17:21; Matthew 28:18-20; Psalm 23:12**)

God's Kingdom and God's Revealed Will

<u>Your Will be done</u> – on earth as it is in Heaven. The Revealed Will of God. The secret will cannot be resisted. God's will must be done.

We must do His Will on earth as it is done in Heaven. The Holy Spirit is given to help us accomplish His Revealed Will for us (**Deuteronomy 29:29**). The secret things belong unto the Lord, our God, but the things which are revealed belong to us and to our children forever, that we may do all of the words of this law. He that wills to do the will of the Father who is in heaven will enter the Kingdom of Heaven (**Matthew 7:21**). We must do God's will and the pleasure of God, as Jesus did and said in **John 5:30**. But, he who does the will of God and carries out His Purpose in his life abides (remains) forever (**First John 2:17b; Psalm 23:3-4**)

Daily Needs

<u>Give us this day our daily bread</u>. God allows us to know that man doesn't live by bread alone, but, by every word of God, that proceeds out of the mouth of the Lord. (**Deuteronomy 8:36**) The provisions of life are given o us by God. (**Ecclesiastes 9:7**) Go your way, eat your bread with joy. (**Psalm 23:5**)

My Daily Bread – Jesus Christ

But it is My father who gives you the true Heavenly Bread. (**John 6:32-35; Psalm 23:5; Ezekiel 34:14-16**). Then they said to Him Lord give us this bread always (all the time)! Our Father gives us our daily bread always and we praise Him for the natural bread for our bodies and for the spiritual Bread of God who came down from heaven and is the Bread of Life for our spirits. I am the Bread of Life (that gives life-the Living Bread). If anyone eats of this Bread, he will live forever. (**John 6:48–51**)

Ask for Forgiveness from God

And forgive us our debts, as we also have forgiven (left remitted) and let go of the debs and have given up resentment against our debtors (**Matthew 6:12**) Forgive people when they are against you. If you do, your Father who is in Heaven will also forgive you. But if you do not forgive people their sin, Your Father will not forgive your sin.

I Forgive Others so God Forgives Me (Psalm 23:5)

And when stand praying, forgive, if ye have ought against any; that your Father also which is in heaven, forgive you your trespasses (**Mark 11:25**). And lead (bring) us not into temptation, but deliver us from the evil one. Him hath God exalted with his right hand to a Prince and a Savior for to give repentance to Israel and forgiveness of sins.

The Kingdom Come (Psalm 23:6)

FOR YOURS IS THE KINGDOM AND THE POWER AND THE GLORY FOREVER, AMEN

The Word of the Lord Concerning the Attainment through Christ of Salvation in The Kingdom of God (Acts 12:24)

Acts 1:3: To them also He showed Himself alive after His passion (His suffering in the garden and on the cross) by (a series of) many convincing demonstrations (unquestioned-evidences and infallible proofs) appearing to them during forty days and talking (to them) about the things of the Kingdom of God.

Acts 2:18: Yes, and on My Menservants also and on My Maidservants in those days, I will pour out My Spirit, and the they shall prophecy telling forth the divine counsels and predicting future events pertaining especially to God's kingdom.

Acts 6:7: And the message of God kept on spreading and the number of disciples multiplied greatly in Jerusalem; and (besides) a large number of the priests were obedient to the faith (in Jesus as the Messiah through whom is obtained eternal salvation in the Kingdom of God.

Acts 8:4: Now those who were scattered abroad went about through the land form place to place) preaching the glad tidings the Word (the doctrine concerning the attainment through Christ of Salvation in the Kingdom of God.

Act 11:19	Acts 14: 22–25,27	Acts 1: 8–10,20
Acts 12:24	Acts 15:7–9,35	Acts 20:25
Acts 13:5	Acts 16:32	Acts 28:23.31
Acts 13:7	Acts 17:11–13	Acts 13:44
Acts 18:11		

Good News Revelations of End Times

(The Gospel of the Kingdom,
The Word of the Lord)

Second Peter 3:3 11: To begin with, you must know and understand this, that scoffers (mockers) will come in the last days with scoffing, (people who) walk after their own fleshly desires. And say, Where is the promise of His coming? For since the forefathers fell asleep, all things have continued exactly as they did from the beginning of creation. For they willfully overlook and forget this (fact) that the heavens came into existence long ago by the <u>Word of God,</u> and the earth and by means of water. Through which the world that then (existed) was deluged with water and perished. (**Genesis 1:6–8; 7:11**). But by the same word the present heavens and earth have been stored up (reserved) for fire, being kept until the day of judgement and destruction of the ungodly people. Nevertheless, do not let this one fact escape you, beloved, that with the Lord one day is as a thousand years and a thousand years as one day. (**Psalm 90:4**) The Lord does not delay and isn't tardy or slow about what He promises, according to some people's conception of slowness, but He is longsuffering (extraordinarily patient) toward you, not desiring that any should perish, but that all should turn to repentance. But the Day of the Lord will come like a thief, and then the heavens will vanish (pass away) with a thunderous crash and the (material) elements (of the universe) will be dissolved with fire, and the earth and the works that are upon it will be burned up. Since all these things are thus in the process of being dissolved, what kind of person ought (each of) you to be in the (meanwhile) in consecrated and holy behavior and devout godly qualities. (**Second Peter 3: 5–15, 18**)

Gospel of the Kingdom of God
(Expect the Word of God to Bless You!)

<u>Read the Word as if Jesus is standing, in front of you as your best friend.</u>

Romans 8:14: FOR ALL WHO ARE LED BY THE SPIRIT OF GOD ARE SONS OF GOD.

1. **Direction** – The way you should go, cause to move or to follow, a certain course. along which something or someone moves to order, show someone the way. Supervision:

   Proverbs 3:6   **Psalms 37:23**

   <u>*Direct*</u> – Your heart to the Lord and serve him only:

   Second Chronicles 29:18: O Lord, God of Abraham, Isaac and Israel, our fathers, keep forever such purpose and thoughts in the minds of Your people, and <u>direct</u> and establish their hearts toward you.

   Psalm 37:23: The steps of a (good) ma are <u>directed </u>an established by the Lord when He delights in his way (and He busiest Himself with his every step).

   Psalm 86:11: *<u>Direct </u>and unite my heart*

Psalm 119:5: Oh, that my ways were <u>directed</u> and established to observe your status (hearing, receiving, loving, and obeying them)!

Proverbs 2:2   **Isaiah 40:13**

First Samuel 7:3c   **Isaiah 45:13**

Proverbs 16:9   **Jeremiah 10:25**

2. **Protection** – shield from injury:

    Psalm 3:3: But You, O Lord, are a <u>shield</u> for me, my glory, and the lifter of my head.

    Psalms 5:12: For You, Lord, will bless the (uncompromisingly) righteous (him who is upright and in right standing with You); as with a <u>shield</u> You will <u>surround</u> him with goodwill (pleasure and favor).

    Psalm 7:10: My defense and <u>shield</u> depends on God. Who saves the upright in heart.

    Ephesian 6:16: Lift up over all the (covering) <u>shield</u> of saving faith, upon which you can quench all the flaming missiles of the wicked (one).

    Genesis 15:1   **Deuteronomy 33:29**

    Psalm 18:35   **Psalm 28:7**

    Psalm 33:20   **Psalm 59:11**

    Psalm 84:9   **Psalm 89:18**

    Psalm 115:10

3. **Perfection** – highest degree of excellence without fault or defect, to make perfect to complete.

Job 11:7: Can you find out the deep things of God, or can you by searching find out the limits of the Almighty, (explore His depths, ascend to His heights, extend to His breadths, and comprehend His infinite perfections)?

Genesis 17:1: And live habitually before Me and be perfect – high degree of excellence; live without fault or defect.

Psalms 138:8	**Luke 8:14**
Hebrew 6:1	**First Peter 2:9**

Correction – Make right, chastise true or factual conforming to a standard

Job 5:17: Happy and fortunate is the man whom God reproves; so, do not despise or reject the correction of the Almighty (subjecting you to trial and suffering).

Job 37:13	**Job 5:17**
Proverbs 3:11	**Hebrew 12:5,6–12**
Proverbs 23:12	**Habakkuk 1:12**
Second Timothy 3:16	

Holy Spirit
(The Promised Blessing)

Galatians 3:14	Galatians 4:6
Second Corinthians 13:14	Ephesians 1:13
Ephesian 4:30	Revelations 14:13b

The Holy Spirit is the Power of the Godhead. The Holy Spirit is the Third Person of the Godhead. Father, Son, Holy Spirit, This is not to minimize His Deity. There is the equality of **ONE**. They are all **ONE.**

The Holy Spirit was, before the beginning of time.

Genesis 1:2-3: And the Spirit of God was hovering over the face of the waters. Then God said, "Let there be light; and there was light."

The Spirit of God was moving (hovering, brooding over the face of the waters (**Genesis 1:2**). The Power of the Spirit is like a thread running throughout the biblical covenant. He shows up in **Genesis 6:3** where *the Lord said, My Spirit shall not forever dwell and strive with man, for he also is flesh; but his days shall yet be 120 years.*

John 6:63: He is the Spirit Who gives life. He is the Life Giver.

John 14:16-17: He is the Comforter (Counselor, Helper, Intercessor, Advocate, Strengthener, and Standby) that He may remain with you forevermore. The Spirit of Truth, He lives with you, and He lives in you (constantly).

First Corinthians 6:19: Your body is His temple. *Do you not know that your body is the temple (the very sanctuary) of the Holy Spirit who lives within you, whom you have received (as a Gift) from God? You are not your own.*

Hebrew 3:6-15: But Christ (the Messiah) was faithful over His (own Father's) House as a Son (and Master of it). And it is we who are now members of this house, if we hold <u>fast and firm to the end</u> our joyful and exultant confidence and sense of triumph in our hope (in Christ). Therefore, as the Holy Spirit says, Today, if you will hear His voice. Do not harden your hearts, as (happened) in the rebellion (of Israel) and their provocation and embitterment (of Me) in the day of testing in the wilderness. Where your fathers tried (My patience) and tested (My forbearance) and found I stood their test, and they saw My works for forty years. And so, I was provoked (displeased and sorely grieved) with that generations, and said. They always err and are led astray in their hearts, and they have not perceived or recognized My ways and become progressively better and more experimentally and intimately acquainted with them. Accordingly, I swore in My wrath and indignation, They shall not enter into My rest. But instead warn (admonish, urge, and encourage) one another every day, as long as it is called Today, that none of you may be hardened (into settled rebellion) by the deceitfulness of sin (by the fraudulence the stratagem, the trickery which the delusive glamor of his sin may play on him. For we have become <u>fellows </u>with Christ (the <u>Messiah</u>) and share in all He has for us, if only we hold our first newborn confidence and original assured expectation (in virtue of which we are believers) firm and unshaken to the end. Then while it is (still) called Today, if you would hear His voice and when you hear it, do not harden your hearts as in the rebellion (in the desert, when the people provoked and irritated and embittered God against them).

We need the (power of the Holy Spirit) if we are to <u>expand</u> the Kingdom of God. Work of expanding the Kingdom of God in you. To make the knowledge of the (King and His Kingdom) – plain and clear so that (he) that readeth may run and <u>do</u> the work of God. (**Ephesians 6:6; Hebrew 4:13**)

Matthew 28:16-20: Then the eleven (11) disciples went to Galilee. They went to the mountain where Jesus had told them to go. When they saw him, they worshipped Hm, but some still had their doubts. Then Jesus came to them. He said, "All authority in Heaven and on Earth has been given to me. So, you must, Go! And make disciples of all nations. Baptizing them into the Name of the Father and of the Son and of the Holy Spirit. Teaching them to observe everything that I have commanded you and behold. I am with you all the days (perpetually, uniformly, and on every occasion) to the (very) close and consummation of the age. Amen (so be it)

This is the assignment given to every believer, to **<u>Go</u>** and do the work of advancing, revealing, and expanding the Kingdom of God (**Matthew 28:19**)

John 1:18: No man has ever seen God at any time; the only unique Son, or the only begotten God. Who is in the bosom (in the intimate presence) of the Father. He has declared Him (He has revealed Him and brought Him out where He can be seen. He has interpreted Him, and He has made Him known).

Mark 16:15: **<u>Go</u>** into all the world and preach and publish openly the good news (the Gospel) to every creature (of the whole human race). And they went out and preached everywhere, while the Lord kept working with the and confirming the message by the attesting signs and miracle that closely accomplished (it). Amen (so be it).

Acts 1:1: In the former account (which I prepared) O Theophilus. I made (a continuous report) dealing with all the things which Jesus began to do and to teach.

Luke1:1-2: Since (as is well known) many have undertaken to put in order and drawings a (through) narrative of the surely established deeds which have been accomplished and fulfilled in and among us. Exactly as they were handed down to us by those who from the (official) beginning (of Jesus' ministry) were eyewitness and ministers of the Word (that is, of "<u>the doctrine concerning the attainment <u>through</u> Christ of Salvation of the Kingdom of God</u>.)

Acts 1:2: Until the day when He ascended, after He – through the Holy Spirit had instructed and commanded the apostles (special messengers) whom He had chosen. To them also He showed Himself alive after His passion (His suffering in the garden and on the cross) by (a series of) many convincing demonstrations, (unquestionable evidences and infallible proofs,) appearing to them during forty days and talking (to them) about the things of the Kingdom of God. And while being in their company and eating at the table with them, He commanded them not to leave Jerusalem but to wait for what the Father had promised of which (He said) you have heard Me speak (**John 14:16;26; 15:26**)

The Gospel of the Kingdom
Manifestation of Holy Spirit God's Power in the Kingdom

Acts 1:5-6: For John baptized with water but not many days from now you shall be baptized with (placed in, introduced unto) the Holy Spirit. So, when they were assembled, they asked Him, Lord, is this the time when You will reestablish the kingdom and restore it to Israel?

Acts !:8: But you shall receive power (ability, efficiency, and <u>might)</u> when the Holy spirit has come upon you, and you shall be my <u>witnesses</u> in Jerusalem and all Judea and Samaria and to the ends of the very bounds of the earth.

His super to our natural becomes supernatural Power of God in us which is the Holy Spirit residence in us.

Acts 1:13-14: And when they had entered (the city) they mounted (the stairs) to the upper room where they were staying. Peter and John and James and Andrew, Philip and Thomas, Bartholomew and Matthew, James son of Alphaeus and Simon the Zealot, and Judas (son) of James. All of these with their minds in full agreement, <u>devoted, themselves steadfastly to prayers,</u> (waiting together) with the women and Mary the Mother of Jesus and with His brothers.

Acts 2:1-4: And when the day of Pentecost had fully come, they were all assembled together in one place. When suddenly there came a sound from Heaven like the rushing of a violent tempest blast, and it filled the whole house in which they were sitting. And there appeared to them tongues resembling fire, which were separated and distributed, and which settled on each one of them. And they were all filled (diffused, throughout their souls) with the Holy Spirit and began to speak in other (different, foreign languages) tongues as the Spirit kept giving them clear and loud expression (in each tongue in appropriate word).

The Holy Spirit comes to give you "Power". Power to live right, power to be right, power to pray right and the Power that only God (himself) can give to a man or woman, to overcome every obstacle, every test, trail or temptation that may get in your way. He, God the Holy Spirit gives joy unspeakable to overcome as you count it all joy. (**James 1:2**)

God gives His power to (us) His people to do the work of the Lord. Preach The acceptable year of the Lord. <u>Good News</u> - the Gospel of the Kingdom of God. <u>To announce</u> – release to the captives and recovery of sight to the blind, to send forth as delivered those who are oppressed (who are downtrodden, bruised, crushed and broken down by calamity). To proclaim when salvation and the free favors of God profusely abound.(**Luke 4:18-19**).

Second Peter 1:21: For no prophecy every originated because some man willed it (to do so – it never came by human impulse), but men spoke from God who were borne along (moved and impelled) by the Holy Spirit.

The Fruit of the Spirit
(Power in the Kingdom of God)

The Characteristics of God in man's spirit developed by walking in the Holy Spirit.

LOVE   PEACE   KINDNESS

JOY   PATIENCE (Longsuffering)   GOODNESS

FAITHFULNESS (faith)

GENTLENESS (meekness, humility) TEMPERANCE (self-control)

The Work which His Holy Spirit presence within accomplishes.

God's character:

LOVE – AGAPE'
(The Amazing Love of God)

John 3:16: For God so greatly <u>loved</u> and dearly prized the world that He (even) gave up His only begotten (unique) Son, so that whosoever believes in (trust in, clings to, relies on) Him shall not perish (come to destruction, be lost) but have eternal (everlasting) life.

Agape – To love without any sound or known reason – unconditionally given. Why does God love me? No reason that I, have been able to figure out His love for me does not exist because of any wonderful thing I am; not even because of some wonderful thing I have done; not because of something I may do. God loves me because he is – AGAPE' <u>LOVE</u>. His love has no conditions, Beauty will not get it, being good does not get it, obedience will not warrant the love God has to give. Sure, all of these are good to have and do, but God's Son died for all- without conditions, While we were yet sinners He died. Jesus shed His precious blood for all mankind. You are included. He desired for us – a pardon – from the Father, so that we could live in peace forever with Him in the Kingdom of God.

Ephesians 3:17-19	**Second Corinthians 13:11**
Romans 13:8	**First Corinthians 12**

THE LORDS OVERFLOWING VICTORY EXPRESSED

First Corinthians 2:8	**Romans 15:13**
First Corinthians 15:57	**Hebrew 1:3**

(The work which His (Holy Spirit) presence within accomplishes)

Love

Live

Out

Victory

Everyday

Amazingly

My

Almighty

Zealously Inspired Name Gives Life and Offers Victory Eternal

Psalm 31:7	Proverbs 3:12	Jeremiah 31:3
Psalms 94:26	Proverbs 17:17	John 5:42
Psalms 6:4	Isaiah 54:8,10	John 5:44
Psalm 25:7	Hosea 14:3	John 5:12
Psalm 25:10	Malachi 1:2	First John 3:1
Psalm 91:14	Psalm 145:20	

John 15:13*:* No greater love than this: That a man would lay down his life for a friend

No one has greater <u>love</u> no one has shown stronger affection) than to lay down (give up) his own life for his friends...Jesus did!

John 3:16: For God so greatly <u>loved</u> and dearly prized the world that He (even) gave up His only begotten (unique) Son so that whosoever believes in (trust in, clings to, relies on) Him shall not perish (come to destruction, be lost) but shall have eternal (everlasting) life.

God sent His Son to save all mankind, no one else could do it, "but the Savior of all, Jesus Christ. Only a Loving, Holy, Majestic, Magnificent, God could love so greatly and did love so perfectly – to live 33 years on earth as a human being; and in finality, He was scorned, rebuked, beaten, spit on, forsaken, harassed, lied to and lied on, rejected, alone, despised, strickened, smitten, afflicted, bruised, pierced, killed and in a borrowed tomb. What <u>Love</u>!! But that is not the end of the story it's really "the beginning". The Amazing Love of God in Christ. He arose! He is Alive!

Charity – benevolence, liberality in thinking and judging, liberality in giving, acts of kindness.

Amazing Love

His amazing love, His amazing love, is all I need to live from above,
No Greater love than this, that He gave his life on the tree
And made the way for you and for me.

How marvelous is His love, Oh, Oh, His love is so amazing
Praise his Name, Oh, praise His Name
Neither worldly fortune nor worldly fame, can be above His precious Name.

Nothing more could He do, He did it all for me and for you
His Name is Jesus, Jesus Christ, He paid the price and gave His life, as the perfect sacrifice.

Now all of us can be free, We can have-the victory!
Through His amazing love, on Calvary, He made the way for me to
Be Free – with His amazing love.

It's amazing, It's amazing, the love God shed on me
Everlasting, Everlasting, It came from above to be, His amazing love, His amazing love.

Jesus, our Yes and Amen!

Joy

The Work which His (Holy Spirit) <u>presence</u> within accomplishes.
God's character in you: the Fruit of the Spirit

Nehemiah 8:10: Then (Ezra) told them, Go your way eat the fat: drink the sweet drink, and send portions to him for whom nothing is prepared; for this day is holy to our Lord. And be not grieved and depressed, <u>for the joy of the Lord</u> is your <u>strength</u> and <u>stronghold</u>.

What is <u>Joy</u>? Delight, happiness, gladness, gleesome, cheerfulness, exultation, gratitude and with great pleasure, enrapture.

Acts 2:28: You will enrapture me (diffused my soul with joy) and within your presence.

Psalms 16:11: You will show me the path of life, in Your presence is fullness of <u>joy</u>, at Your right hand there are pleasures, forevermore.

Psalms 51:8: Make me to hear <u>joy</u> and <u>gladness</u> and be satisfied; let the bones which You have broken rejoice.

Psalms 126:5: *They who sow in tears shall reap in <u>joy</u> and singing.*

John 15:11: This thing I have spoken to you that <u>my joy</u> may remain in you; and that your <u>joy</u> may be full.

John 17:13: And now I am coming to you; I say these things while I am still in this world, so that <u>my joy</u> may be made full and complete and perfect <u>in them</u> that my enjoyment many be perfected in their own souls, that they may have my gladness within them, filling their hearts. **(James 1:2)**

The Fullness of <u>Joy</u>

<u>JOY</u> TO THE WORLD! JESUS IS COMING SOON! HE IS ALIVE!

He hears your voice when you pray. Hope in God wait patiently on Him expectantly on Him

Psalms 42 **Isaiah 42** **Romans 8:19-28**

He is Alive!

Peace

He hears your sincere voice when you pray.

Hope in God waits patiently on him, expectantly on him.

Psalms 42   **Isaiah 42**   **Romans 8:19-28**

Perfectly Enriched at Christ's Expense. (the work which His presence within accomplished).

James 3:17-18; Second Peter 1:2 God's character in you:

We have a Father who is a _peace_ giving God. He sent His only begotten Son to allow His sons (adopted) to realize the possibility of _peace_. Your peace was (is) assured by Christ when He died on Mount Calvary and rose again. For He is (Himself) our _Peace_ (**Ephesian 2:14**). Now may the God of Peace (which is the Author and the Giver of _Peace_). Who brought again from among the dead our Lord Jesus (**Hebrew 23:20**). After all the _Kingdom of God_ is not a matter (of getting) the food and drink (one likes) but instead it is righteousness (that state which makes a person acceptable to God) and (heart) _peace_ and _joy_ in the Holy Spirit (**Romans 14:17**).

Ephesians 2:19: And He came and preached the glad tidings of _peace_ to you who were afar off and (peace) to those who were near.

Isaiah 57:19a: _Peace, Peace,_ to his who is far off (both Jew and Gentile) and to him who is near! says the Lord.

Second Corinthians 13:11: _The author and promoter of peace will be with you._

What is Peace? According to Webster dictionary and Strong's Concordance – it a state of calm and quiet, absence of war or strife, be quiet, security or ease, safe, well, to refrain from worry or depression, deliverance, good health, to make restitution, restore, make good, (re) pay (pay again), prosper(ous).

Psalms 119:165: Great <u>peace</u> have they who love Your law, nothing shall offend them or make them stumble.

Isaiah 32:17: And the effect of righteousness will be <u>peace</u> (internal and external) and the result of righteousness will be quietness and confident trust forever.

Zechariah 8:12a: For these shall the <u>seed</u> produce <u>peace</u> and <u>prosperity</u>. The <u>seed</u> is the Word of God spoken by the believer in assurance that the promises are given with a Yea! And Amen (Yes and <u>so</u> <u>be it</u>).

Hebrew 12:14: Strive to live in <u>peace</u> with everybody and pursue that connection and holiness without which no one will (ever) see the Lord.

Psalm 37:11: But the meek (in the end) shall inherit the earth and shall delight themselves in the abundance of <u>peace.</u>

Patience
(Longsuffering)

Galatians 5:22	**Colossians 3:12**
James 1:12	**First Timothy6:11**
Ephesians 4:2	**Second Timothy 3:10**
Colossians 1:11	**Hebrews 10:36**
Titus 2:2	

(The work which His Holy Spirit presence within accomplishes). Bearing pain or trials without complain habit of being <u>patient</u>. (Webster dictionary) to be forbearing, fortitude, endurance, constancy, mild, gentle, preserving, bearing long, trials, trouble, and test with good temper. (Strong's Dictionary).

James 1:12: Blessed (happy to be envied) is the man who is <u>patient</u> under trail and stands up under temptation, for when he has stood the test and been approved, he will receive (the victor's) crown of life which God has promised to those who love him.

But as for that (seed) in the good soil, these are (the people) who, hearing the Word, hold it fast in a just (noble, virtuous) and worthy heart, and steadily bring forth fruit with <u>patience</u>.

James 1:3-4: Be assured and understand that the trial and proving of your faith bring out endurance and steadfastness and <u>patience.</u>

But let endurance and steadfastness and <u>patience</u> have full play and do a thorough work, so that you may be (people) perfectly and fully developed (with no defects), lacking in nothing.

Matthew 5:5: Blessed (happy, blithesome, joyous, spiritually prosperous with life, joy and satisfaction in God's favor and salvation, regardless of their outward condition) are the mark (the mild, <u>patient</u>, long-suffering) for the shall inherit the earth.

Kindness

Kindness is favor, affection, benevolence, moral excellence.

Law of Kindness – blessing someone with counsel and instruction. This is an act of kindness. kindness is something that has to be given to someone. When you are kind to one another you are willing to give as much as you can, to allow the person to know, feel and to have this as your character action.

Kindness is a twin affection with love which is the principal characteristic of God. The grace or favor of God; His unmerited favor, a merciful kindness. Kindness is a fruit of the Holy Spirit: It is given through our Lord Jesus Christ for we receive kindness, "gracious generosity". His undeserved favor and spiritual blessings. Jesus Christ is the Vine, and the Father is the Vine dresser. We (the Christian) are the branches, the fruit comes on the branches, but the nourishments comes through the Vine. Jesus said in **John15:4**, "Just *as a branch cannot bear fruit of itself without abiding in (being vitally united to) the vine, neither can you bear fruit unless you abide in Me"*, *V.5: I am the vine; You are the branches. Whoever lives is Me and I in him bears much (abundant) fruit. However, apart from Me (cut off from vital union with me) you can do nothing.* We must be wealthy with the fruit of kindness and forbearance and longsuffering, patience. Father God promised David, as a part of the everlasting covenant, (kindness, goodwill, and compassion), kindness is to be passed on as God grows and prospers this fruit (His character action) in you. You must pass it on to someone it is not a fruit for you to enjoy alone, it must be given to others. These fruits are to bear or carry over to others, to render or give something to benefit others. To profit or prosper from someone being kind and compassionate to others. Put on therefore, as the elect of God, holy and beloved, bowels of mercies.

Second Samuel 9:3	**Galatians 5:22**	**Proverbs 31:26**
Second Corinthians 8:9	**Proverbs 19:22**	**Psalm 141:5**
Isaiah 54:8	**Second Samuel 16:17**	**Isaiah 54:10**

Colossians 3:12: *Kindness, humbleness of mind, meekness, longsuffering*

"Let kindness be the rule for everything you do or say."

Goodness

Nehemiah 9:35	Zechariah 9:17
Psalm 27:13	Second Corinthians 9:9
Psalm 31:19	Ephesians 15:14
Psalm 145:7	Romans 15:14
Hosea 6:6	Exodus 33:19

Well-behaved, kind, good, favor, virtue, beneficence, moral excellence, welfare, to make, to be a well-doer, good repute, benevolence, to do for the benefit of others. Goodness is virtuous, a character fruit of God.

Exodus 33:19a: And God said, I will make all My goodness pass before you, and I will proclaim My name, THE LORD, before you.

They did not serve you in their kingdom, and in Your great goodness that you have them and in the large and rich land You set before them nor did they turn from their wicked ways.

Psalm 27:13: (What would have become of me) had I not believed that I would see the Lord's goodness in the land of the living!

Psalm 112:9: As it is written, He (the benevolent person) scatters abroad, He gives to the poor; His deeds of justice and goodness and kindness and benevolence will go on and endure forever.

Ephesians 5:9: For the fruit (the effect, the product) of the Light or the Spirit (consists) in every form of kindly goodness uprightness of heart, and trueness of life.

Faithfulness

Faithfulness – Fidelity, steadiness, certainty, truth, to render sure, proper stability establish, fix, prosperous.

Deuteronomy 32:4: He is the Rock. His work is perfect, for all His ways are low, and justice. A God of faithfulness without breach or deviation just and right is He.

First Samuel 26:23a: *The lord rewards every man for his righteousness and his faithfulness;*

Psalm 25:10: All the paths of the Lord are mercy and steadfast love, even truth and faithfulness are they for those who keep his covenant and His testimonies.

Psalms 119:30: I have chosen the way of truth and faithfulness: Your ordinances have I set before me.

Hosea 2:20: I will even betroth you to Me in stability and in faithfulness and you shall know (recognize, be acquainted with, appreciate give heed to and cherish the Lord.

Galatians 5:22	**Psalm 88:11**	**Psalm 89:1,8,33**
Psalm 91:4	**Psalm 92:2**	**Psalm 108:4**
Psalm 117:2	**Psalm 119:73**	**Psalm 119:90**
Psalm 143:1	**Isaiah 11:5**	**Lamentations 3:23**

Gentleness
(Meekness, Humility)

Gentleness – of a family of high social station, not harsh, stern, or violent, soft or delicate.

Proverbs 18:35 – You have also given me the shield of your salvation, and your right hand has held me up. Your gentleness and condescension have made me great.

First Corinthians 4:20 – For the Kingdom of God consists of and is based on not talk but power (moral power and excellence of soul)

First Corinthians 4:21 – Now which do you prefer? Shall I come to you with a rod or correction, or with love and in a spirit of gentleness.

Galatians 6:7 – Brethren, if any person is overtaken in misconduct or sin of any sort, you who are spiritual (who are responsive to and controlled by the spirit) should set him right and restore and reinstate him, without any sense of superiority and with all gentleness, keeping an attentive eye on yourself lest you should be tempted also.

Ephesians 4:2

Second Timothy 5:25

Colossians 3:12-13

Hebrew 5:21

First Peter 3:4 - It should be that of your inner self, the unfading beauty of a gentle and quiet spirit, which is of great worth in God's sight.

Numbers 12:3 – Now the man Moses was very meek (gentle, kind, and humble) or above all the men on the face of the earth.

Proverbs 15:4 – A gentle tongue (with its healing power) is a tree of life, but willful contrariness in it breaks down the spirit.

Matthew 11:29 – Take My yoke upon you and learn of me, for I am <u>gentle</u> (meek) and humble (lowly) in heart, and you will fine rest (relief and ease and refreshment and recreation and blessed quiet) for your souls.

Temperance
(Self-Control, Self-Restraint)

The observance of moderation temperateness moderation in regard to the indulgence of the natural appetites and passions; restrained or moderate indulgence, sobriety, sometimes loosely used to mean total abstinence from intoxicants, reasonable calm. Disposition or constitution of the mind with regard to the passion and affections, control exercised over one's self to hold back to hold in, to check, to restrict, a limitation.

First Timothy 3:2a: Now a bishop (superintendent, overseer) must give no grounds for accusation but must be above reproach, the husband of one wife circumspect and temperate and self-controlled:

First Timothy 1:7: For God did not give us a spirit of timidity (of cowardice of craven and cringing and fawning fear), but (He has given us a spirit) of power and of love and of calm and well-balanced mind and discipline and self-control.

Second Peter 1:6: And in (exercising) knowledge (develop) self-control, and in (exercising) self-control. (develop) steadfastness (patience, endurance) and in (exercising) brotherly affection (develop) Christian love.

Proverbs 19:11: Good sense make a man restrain his anger, and it is his glory to overlook a transgression of an offense.

Proverbs 1:15
Proverbs 10:19
Romans 7:9

Kingdom Principles
(Invisible Kingdom – God is a Spirit)

Principle of Service: Luke 1:74-75 – *You must serve,* Jesus said it.
Principle of Giver: Luke 6:38 – *You must give, and it will be given to you*
Principle of Use (Unity): *You must use it or lose it.*

Principle of Reciprocity: Second Corinthians 8:10 – *Give and it will be given to you*

Matthew 7:12: *Do unto others as you would have them do to you.*

Galatians 5:13: *Through love, you should serve one another.*

1. *Love God with all you heart and with all your soul and with all your mind.*

   For the whole law (concerning human relationships is compiled with in the one precept.

2. *You shall love, your neighbor as (you do) yourself.*

Psalms 139:21-22   **Leviticus 19:18**   **Matthew 5:43-46**

Plans and Purpose of God: Who can stop it: THE INTENDED REASON

First Chronicles 29:18	**Proverbs 12:4**	**Proverbs 12:8**
Isaiah 14:26-27	**Isaiah 46:10–11**	**Acts 5:38–39**
Hebrew 6:17–20	**Proverbs 20:18**	**Isaiah 55:11**
John 12:27	**Romans 8:28**	**Ephesian 3:10-11, 21**

We are His children; we must trust God with our everything. He knows the way, He knows the truth, and He knows (this) life.

Johns 14:6: In fact, Jesus said, "I am the Way and the Truth and the Life: no one comes to the Father except by (through) me

Plan: Method for accomplishing something – THE INTENT.

Purpose: Something (as a result) aimed at. INTENT

Kingdom of God

Principles of the Kingdom – Servant Giver

The Reward of Service: Always Serve.

Luke 10:36: Which of these three do you think proved himself a neighbor to him who fell among robbers.

v.37: He answered, The one who showed pity and mercy to him. And Jesus said to him, Go and do likewise.

Jesus shows His love for us in the same way as this Samaritan did in this story. He is moved with pity and mercy for every one of us. He picks us up from wherever the robber (the thief, devil, and demons spirits) have stripped us of our self-esteem, love, peace, happiness, family, money, and in every other way (as Sinners) we find ourselves (drugs, alcohol, and secret sins). He brings us to the inn (the Father's house) and binds our wounds and paid for our keep, and takes good care of us. He leads us to His saving knowledge and says (paid) for our sins and shortcomings. His sacrifice on Calvary and His blood pays (paid) the price for every sinner.

Whatever more is required, the Holy Spirit comes in until Jesus returns, He is our Comforter, Counselor, Helper. Intercessor, Advocate, Strengthener and Standby.

John 14:16: *That he may remain with you forever.* He is the Spirit of Truth.

John 14:18: *He never leaves us as orphans (comfortless) desolate bereaved, forlorn helpless).* I will come back to you.

Luke 10:28: Jesus said, "We will live (enjoy, active, blessed, endless life in the Kingdom of God.)

Matthew 9:35-38: Gift of God

Plan and Purpose of God for the Kingdom of God

Ephesians 3:8: To me, though I am the very least of all the saints (God's consecrated people). This grace (favor, privilege) was granted and graciously entrusted; to proclaim to the Gentiles the unending (boundless, fathomless, incalculable, and exhausted) riches of Christ (wealth which no human being could have searched out.

V.9: Also, to enlighten all men and make plain to them what is the <u>plan</u> (regarding the Gentiles and providing for the salvation of all men) of the mystery kept hidden through the ages and concealed until <u>now</u> (in the mind of <u>God</u>, Who created all things.

V.10: (The purpose is) that through the <u>church</u> the complicated many- sided wisdom of God in all its infinite variety and innumerable aspects might now be made known to the angelic rulers and authority (principalities and powers) in the heavenly sphere.

V.11: This is in accordance with the terms of the eternal and timeless <u>purpose</u> which He has realized and carried into effect in (the person of) Christ Jesus our Lord.

V.12: In whom, because of our faith in Him, we dare to have the boldness (courage and confidence) of free access (an unreserved approach to God with freedom and without fear).

Hebrews 4:16: Let us then fearlessly and confidently and boldly draw near to the throne of Grace (the throne of God's unmerited favor to us sinners), that we may receive mercy (for our failures) and find grace to help in good time for every need (appropriate help and well-timed help, coming just when we need it).

<u>God wanted a family</u>: His plan (intent) and purpose (intend, aimed at) to have as a plan and to concentrate on this one purpose. God wanted a family, and He fixed His attention on that. God interacts with man from the beginning God had a relationship with man according to

the historical account in Genesis (a Greek word meaning origins" or beginning". The Hebrew text reads "<u>Bereshith</u>" which means "In the beginning").

After the creation of the heavens and the earth, the Spirit of God moved over the face of the waters. God said, "Let there be..." and there was day and night, sun, moon, and stars, God said: and there was (for six days) the whole of creation

Genesis 1:26: God said, "Let us (father, Son, and Holy Spirit) make mankind in Our image, after Our likeness, and let them have complete authority over the fish of the sea, the birds of the air, the (tame) beasts and over all of the earth, and over everything that creeps upon the earth.

What I understand is that God made everything on earth for mankind and all He wanted is fellowship with mankind, He blessed them, gave them food, a garden with everything in it pleasant to ones eyes and told them to take dominion and enjoy.

Genesis 1:28: Be fruitful and multiply and replenish the earth. Subdue the earth (using all its vast resources in the <u>service</u> of God and man). Have dominion over every living creature that moves on the earth.

God blessed the seventh day and rested from all His works. He set apart the seventh day as His own. He hallowed it-the seventh day. His Sabbath!

Proverbs 3:19: *The Lord by skillful and Godly Wisdom has founded the earth; by understanding He has established the heavens* (**Colossians 1:16**)

V.20: By His knowledge the deeps were broken up, and the skies distill the dew.

V.21: My son, let them not escape from your sight, but keep sound and Godly Wisdom and discretion.

V.22: And they will be life to you inner self, and a gracious ornament to your neck (your outer self).

V.23: Then you will walk in your way <u>securely</u> and in <u>confident</u> trust, and you shall not dash your foot or stumble. When you lie down, you shall not be afraid: Yes, you shall lie down, and your sleep shall be sweet.

Grace

Unmerited Favor of God

God's **R**escues **A**nd **C**omfort **E**veryone

God's **R**ighteous **A**bundance **C**ome **E**veryday

God's **R**iches **A**t **C**hrist **E**xpense

Acts 20:24c: Faithfully to attest to the Good News (Gospel) of God's grace (His <u>unmerited</u> <u>favor</u>, spiritual blessing, and mercy).

Ephesians 2:5: Amazing <u>Grace</u> – How sweet the sound that <u>saved</u> a wretch like me!

Psalm 148:56: <u>God rescued and comforted</u> everyone. GRACE for He commanded, and they were created.

Ephesians 2:8-9: *For it is by <u>Grace</u> (His favor and mercy which you did not deserve) that you are saved (delivered from judgement and made partakers of Christ salvation) through your faith.* (**Romans 3:24; Romans 5:20 and Romans 6:14**)

What is Grace?

<u>Webster's Dictionary</u> – Unmerited divine assistance, respite, unmerited favor and mercy. <u>Strong's Dictionary</u> – Well-favored to stoop in kindness to an inferior to bestow, to implore (is move to favor by petition) to have pity upon. READ: **Acts 2:38-44, Galatians 3:13-14, 26,29:**

Proverbs 1:9: A garland of Grace upon your head, Crown. We are to grow in Grace (undeserved favor)

Second Peter 3:18: Spiritual Strength (**Second Peter 1:2**) <u>Grace</u> – the Gift of God

Romans 1:7: *To (you then) all, God's beloved ones in Rome, called to be saints and designated for a consecrated life designated for a consecrated life, <u>Grace</u> and spiritual blessing and peace be yours from God our Father and from the Lord Jesus Christ.* (**Second Peter 3:18; First Peter 5:5; James 4:16; Ephesians 2:5-8; Ephesians 3:8**)

Amazing Grace – How sweet the sound that saved a wretch like me!

Repentance

Romans 2:4: Or are you (so blind as to) trifle with and presume upon and despise and underestimate the <u>wealth</u> of His <u>Kindness</u>, and <u>Forbearance</u> and <u>Longsuffering</u>, <u>Patience</u>? Are you unmindful or actually ignorant (of the fact) that <u>God's Kindness</u> is intended to lead you to repent (<u>to change</u> <u>your mind and inner man to accept God's will?</u>)

Second Peter 3:9: The Lord does not delay and is not tardy or slow about what He promises, according to some people's conception to slowness, but he is long-suffering (extraordinarily patient) toward you, not desiring that any should perish, but that all should turn to repentance.

In order to receive this wonderful <u>Amazing Grace</u>, we must all repent and <u>change our mind</u> and <u>our inner man</u> must be renewed to <u>accept the will of God</u> in our <u>hearts</u> and ask God to come into our lives and be changed into newness of lives.

Salvation
Jesus is the Way!

Galatians 3:22	**Isaiah 12:2-3**	**Galatians 3:13-14**
Hebrew 5:9	**Isaiah 45:21-25**	**Psalm 9:4**
Revelation 7:10	**Isaiah 46:13**	**Psalms 25:5**
Psalms 24:5	**Isaiah 49:6**	

Ephesians 2:5-8 – The Gift of God

Isaiah 45:17 – Salvation of Israel

Salvation – Webster's Dictionary – saving of a person from sin or danger.

Strong's Dictionary – (Y-"shur" ah) deliverance, aid to, make safe, free, liberty, prosperity, rescue, defense, victory, health, help, welfare, victory.

But the scriptures – (**Galatians 3:22**) picture all mankind as sinners.

Galatians 3:13-14: *God purchased our freedom (redeeming us).*

Psalms 25:5: *You are God of my salvation.*

This salvation did not come to us because of anything we have done it came not according to our own striving, but it is the Gift of God!

I bring My righteousness (in the deliverance of Israel), it will not be for off, and My salvation shall not tarry, and I will put salvation in Zion, for Israel My glory (yes, give salvation in Zion and My glory to Israel).

Salvation – Way into the Kingdom of God (Jesus is the Way!)

In order to see God and get into His Kingdom we must be <u>born again</u> or <u>born from above.</u>

Romans 10:8: But what does it say? The Word (God's message in Christ) is near you, on your lips and in your heart, that is the Word (the message, the basis and object) of faith which we preach. (**Deuteronomy 30:14**)

V.9: Because if you acknowledge and confess with your lips that Jesus is Lord and in you heart believe (adhere to, trust in and rely on the truth) that God raised Him from the dead, you will be saved.

<u>Sinner's Prayer</u>

God in Heaven, I come to You in the Name of Jesus. Your Word says, "... Him that cometh to me, I will in no wise cast out (**John 6:37**). So, I know you won't cast me out, but you will take me in, and I thank you for it. You said in Your Word, "...if I shalt confess with my mouth the Lord, Jesus and shalt, believe in my heart that God has raised him from the dead, thou (I) shalt be saved…"(**Romans 10:9**). I am confessing with my mouth, and I believe in my heart that Jesus is the Son Of God and He was raised from the dead for my justification, and I receive Him right now as my Lord and Savior. Thank you, Father, for saving me. In Jesus' name, I Pray.

AMEN.

Salvation – the Way into the Kingdom of God for the Believer

Romans 8:10: For with the heart a person believes (adheres to, trust in, and relies on Christ) and so is justified, (declared righteous, acceptable to God), and with the mouth he confesses (declares openly and speaks out freely his faith) and confirms (his) salvation.

V.11: The scripture says, No man who believes in Him (who adheres to, relies on and trusts in Him) will (ever) be put to shame or be disappointed.

V.12: (No one) for there is no distinction between Jew and Greek. The same Lord is Lord over all (of us) and He generously bestows His riches upon all who call upon Him (in faith).

V.13: For everyone who calls upon the Name of the Lord (evoking Him as Lord) will be saved.

Joel 2:32: And whoever shall call on the Name of the Lord shall be delivered and saved, for in Mount Zion (church) and in Jerusalem there shall be those who escape, as the Lord has said and among the remnant (of survivors) shall be those whom the Lord calls.

Acts 2:17-21   **Romans 10:13-15**

Born Again

Born Again from Heaven above
Born Again by Jesus love
Born Again, Oh, I'm Born Again
Born Again, Born Again

Born Again, Free From Sin
I'm Born Again, Born Again
From Heaven Above and Free Within
Born Again by Jesus Blood
Born into His Heavenly Love
Born, Born Again, Born Again I'm Born Again

I'm a New Creation in Christ
Born into a Relation, He Paid the Price
Born Within and Born Again
Born into the Kingdom of His Love
Born to Live with the Father Up Above
I'm Born Again, Born Again.

Praise

Psalm 145:4	Psalm 31:31	Psalm 138
Psalm 30:9	Psalm 148,149,150	Psalm 139
Psalm 42:5	Psalm 63:3	

Hebrew 13:15*:* By Him therefore let us offer the sacrifice of <u>praise</u> to God continually, that is, the fruit of our lips giving thanks to His Name.

Leviticus 22:29: And when you sacrifice an offering of thanksgiving to the Lord, sacrifice it so that you may be accepted.

A Praise to you

Let my life be a praise to You. In everything that I say and do. Let me life be a praise to You A sweet sacrifice as I kneel at you throne seeking Your face while Your amazing Grace is Shone. Praising You, O Lord, as I seek Your face for You are my righteousness, You are my Soon coming King,

Glory to you, O Lord, for everything. Hallelujah, Hallelujah, Hallelujah! You are my soon coming King. So let my life be a praise to You, In everything that I say and do. Let my life be a praise to You, O, Lord. Let my life's sacrifice be a praise to you.

Praise God for who He is to us, His children and to who He is to the entire creation. He is our life, our breath, our movement, our everything. Praise God from whom all blessing flow.

Exodus 15:2 (ESV)

The Lord is my strength and my song, and
he has become my salvation;
this is my God, and I will praise him,
my father's God, and I will exalt him.

Strength

Habakkuk 3:19: The Lord God is my Strength, my personal bravery and my invincible army; He make my feet like hinds feet and will make me to walk (not to stand still in terror, but to walk) and make (spiritual) progress upon my high places (of trouble, suffering or responsibility).

Strength – quality of being strong, toughness capable of withstanding stress or violence, healthy, grow stronger. Ability, power or force, valor, wealth. **Webster and Strong's Dictionary** – toughness, might and inflexibilities (amp).

Psalms 59:17: God is my <u>Strength</u>, My Defense, My Fortress and High Tower. The God who shows me mercy and steadfast love.

First Peter 4:11: *With the <u>Strength</u> which God furnishes abundantly.*

First Peter 5:10: *Establish and ground you securely, and <u>strengthen</u> and settle you.*

Second Peter 1:10: *To ratify, to strengthen, to make steadfast.*

I have I have <u>strength</u> for all things in Christ who empowers me. (I am ready for anything and equal to anything through Him who infuses <u>strength</u> into me.

My <u>strength</u> makes me self-sufficient in Christ's sufficiency, to be strong and continue as strong, enduring, zealous, healthy, capable of exerting great force or of withstanding stress or violence, toughness.

Second Corinthians 13:9	**Isaiah 40:29 (AMP)**	
Psalms 27:1	**Hebrew 13:21**	**Nehemiah 8:10**
Psalm 28:7	**Psalm 138:3**	**Psalm 118.14**

Luke 10:19 - (physical and mental strength and ability)

Ephesians 3:16: May He grant you out of the rich treasury of His Glory to be <u>strengthened</u> and reinforced with mighty power in the inner man by the (Holy) Spirit (Himself) indwelling your innermost being and personality.

Wisdom
(The Principal Thing)

Psalm 4:5,7	Deuteronomy 4:6	Psalm 111:10
James 3:17-18	Proverb 9:10	Job 28:28
Colossians 1:9	Proverbs 19:8	First Kings 4:29-30
Ephesians 1:17	Colossians 4:5	Proverbs 16:16
Revelations 13:18	Revelations 5:2	

First Corinthians 1:24, 30

SOUND JUDGEMENT: Having the power of discerning and judging correctly, possessed of discernment judgment and (discretion; prudent and sensible; sage; judicious; experienced; skilled; godly, pious in a wise manner (Webster's Dictionary)

Proverbs 1:2: That people may know skilled and Godly <u>Wisdom</u> and instruction, <u>discern</u> and <u>comprehend</u> the words of <u>understanding</u> and <u>insight</u>.

Proverbs 2:4*:* If you seek (<u>Wisdom</u>) as for silver and search for skillful and Godly Wisdom as for hidden treasures.

Proverbs 2:5 –7: Then you will understand the reverent and worshipful fear of the Lord and find the knowledge of (our omniscient) God. He hides away sound and Godly <u>Wisdom </u>and stores it for the righteous (those who are upright and in right standing with Him. He is a shield to those who walk uprightly and in integrity.

The Book of Proverbs is a biblical answer of the impartation of the reason for the reverential fear of the Lord. The skillful and Godly <u>Wisdom</u>. It is a book of practicality dealing with the art of living. The reverence for God is set forth as the path of life and the security of life well lived. <u>Wisdom</u> is being able to discern between good and evil in the everyday life of the believer. To have success in life we must have God's <u>wisdom</u> in our hearts and in our understanding, We need to follow the worthwhile words given in the scriptures to lea us to good success.

Joshua 1:8: This book of the Law shall not depart out of your mouth, but you shall meditate on it day and night that you may observe and do according to all that is written in it. For then you shall make you way prosperous and then you shall deal wisely and have good success.

<u>Wisdom</u> is in the Word and so as you walk in the Word <u>Wisdom</u> comes to you – who applies the Word by living by faith, or by acting on the Word of God. Behold the reverential and worshipful fear of the Lord-that is <u>Wisdom;</u> and the depart from evil is understanding.

Wisdom is-to now the difference in discernment.

The **Proverb 31** - Virtuous woman knew the Wisdom of God. She opens her mouth with wisdom (**Proverbs 31:26**)

Proverbs 31:30: Favour is deceitful, ad beauty in vain; but a woman that feareth the Lord, she shall be praised.

Righteousness

<u>Being right, Upright, Virtuous</u>: Acting in accordance with the dictates of religion or morality; free from guilt or sin. Agreeing with right, just, equitable. The state of being right with God. Having right-standing with God. Webster's Dictionary – beneficence, equity, justification.

<u>The desire to conform to God's Will</u>: To be aware about God and to desire to please Him in character, thoughts, and actions, The will to live by the Word of God.

Genesis 15:6: Abraham believed in (trusted in, relied on remained steadfast to) the Lord, and He (God) counted it to him as <u>righteousness,</u> (right standing) with God.

Psalm 17:15	**Psalm 40:10**	**Psalm 106:31**
Proverbs 10:2	**Isaiah 54:17**	

Galatians 3:6: Thus, Abraham believed in and adhered to and trusted in and relied on God, and it was reckoned and placed to his account and credited as <u>righteousness</u> (as conformity to the divine will in purpose, thought and action).

Genesis 15:6	**Ephesians 4:24**	**James 1:20**
Psalm 24:5	**Proverb 11:6**	**Ephesian 5:9**

Ephesian 6:14

Hebrew 11:7: (Prompted by faith Noah being forewarned by God concerning events of which as yet there was no visible sign took heed diligently and reverently constructed and prepared an ark for the deliverance of his own family. By this (his faith which relied on God) he passed judgment and sentence on the world's unbelief and became an heir and possessor of <u>righteousness</u> (that relation of being right into which God puts the person who has faith). (**Genesis 6:13-22**)

Proverbs 10:2: *<u>Righteousness</u> delivereth from death*

Proverbs 11:6: *<u>Righteousness</u> of upright shall deliver them*

Proverbs 14:34: *<u>Righteousness</u> exalteth a nation.* **Proverbs 21:21:** *The seeker of <u>righteousness</u> will find life.* **Romans 5:17:** *The free gift of <u>righteousness,</u>*

Romans 4:17: The Kingdom of God is not food and drink, but it is <u>righteousness.</u>

Ephesians 5:9: *Fruit of Spirit is <u>righteousness</u>* **Ephesian 6:14:** *Breastplate of <u>righteousness</u>* **Philippians 3:9:** *Not having mine own <u>righteousness</u>*

Titus 3:5: Not by works of <u>righteousness</u> which we have done, but according to his mercy he saved us, by the washing of <u>regeneration</u> and <u>renewing</u> of the Holy Ghost.

James 3:18: And the harvest of <u>righteousness</u> (of conformity to God's will in thought and deed) is (the fruit of the seed) sown in peace (in themselves and in others, that peace which means concord, agreement, and harmony between individuals, with undisturbedness, in a peaceful mind free from fears and agitating passions and moral conflicts).

Genesis 15:6	**Psalms 106:31**	**James 1:20**
Deuteronomy 8:25	**Psalms 24:5**	**Ephesians 4:24**

Honour

Reverence, Value a price paid or received. Preciousness – Sum total.

Proverbs 15:31: He who oppresses the poor reproaches, mocks, and insults his Maker, but he who is kind and merciful to the needy, honors Him.

First Peter 2:7: The honour and inestimable value of Christ as appropriated by believers, by believers, who are joined as living stones to Him the Cornerstone, of the preciousness of Christ unto believers.

Vine's Dictionary: Esteem – used in ascription of worship to God.

First Timothy 1:17: King of Eternity – be honour and glory forever and ever (to the ages of ages) Amen (so be it) bestowed on Christ by the Father.

Hebrews 2:9　　　　**Second Peter 1:17**　　**John 5:23**

Honour- bestowed upon man (**Hebrew 2:7**) to be the reward of patience in well-doing (**Romans 2:7**).

Honour must be given; it cannot be claimed for self.

Second Timothy 2:21: Honour is to be given – and God gives honour to the ones who deserve or earns it because of what Christ did, God values the person who is a (vessel) meet for the Master's use.

To be given by (**First Peter 2:17**) believers one to another (**Romans 12:10**)

First timothy 5:17: To be given to Elders that rule well (double honour) (here the meaning may be an honorarium)

Hebrew 2:7: *God gives* <u>honor</u> *to man and is mindful to him in His Word.* (**Psalm 8:4–6**)

Hebrew 13:4: Let marriage be held in <u>honor</u> (esteemed worthy, precious of great price and especially clears) in all things.

Deuteronomy 26:2: <u>*Honour*</u> *the Lord with your capital and sufficiency (from righteous labors) and with the first fruits of all your income.* (**Malachi 3:10; and Luke 14:13; 14:15**)

Obedience

Second Samuel 22:45: Foreigners yielded feigned <u>obedience</u> to me; as soon as they heard of me, they became <u>obedient</u> to me.

<u>Obedience</u> – Willing to obey or do the command of God and to be a people that are models of the Word of God. Follow the commands and guidance of the Word of God and behave in accordance with His commandments of Love.

Second Corinthians 7:15: And his heart goes out to you more abundantly than ever as he recalls the <u>submission</u> (to his guidance) that all of you had and the reverence and anxiety (to meet all requirements) with which you accepted and welcomed him.

Romans 1:5: It is through him that we have received grace (God's unmerited favor) and (our) apostleship to promote <u>obedience</u> to the faith and make disciples for His Name's sake among all the nations.

Faith is one of the main subjects of the Epistle (Romans) and is the initial act of <u>obedience</u> in the new life, as well.

Romans 15:18: For (of course) I will not venture (presume) to speak thus of any work except what Christ has actually done through me (as an instrument in His Hands) to win <u>obedience</u> from the Gentiles by word and deed.

Romans 16:19: For while your loyalty and <u>obedience</u> is known to all, so that I rejoice over you, I would have you well versed and wise as to what is good and innocent ad guileless as to what is evil.

Romans 16:26: But is now disclosed and this the prophetic scriptures is made known to all nations, according to the command of the eternal God, (to win them) to <u>obedience</u> to the faith.

Second Corinthians 10:5   **Philippians 2:8**   **Hebrew 5:8**

First Peter 1:14   **First Peter 1:22**   **First John 3:6**

If you are willing and <u>obedient</u>, you shall eat the good of the land.

<u>Obey</u> – **First Samuel 15:22**   **Acts 5:29**   **Ephesians 6:1**
                   Colossians 3:22   **Hebrew 13:17**

Faithful

Faithful – Trustworthiness, fidelity, steadiness, reliable, (pistis – Greek)

Strong's dictionary – Credence, conviction of truth, or (the truthfulness of God or a religious teacher) a reliance upon Christ for salvation, constancy in such, profession by extension, the system of religious (Gospel) truth itself – assurance, belief, believes, faith, fidelity.

First Samuel 2:35a: And I will raise up for Myself a faithful priest who shall do according to what is in My heart and mind.

First Samuel 22:14b: *And who is so faithful among all your servants as David.*

Nehemiah 7:2b: For Hananiah was a more faithful and God-fearing man than many.

Psalm 31:23: O, love the Lord, all you, His saints! The Lord preserves the faithful and plentifully pays back him who deals haughtily.

Proverbs 11:13: He who goes about as a talebearer reveals secrets, but he who is trustworthy and faithful in spirit keeps the matter hidden.

First Corinthians 4:2: Moreover, it is (essentially) required of stewards that a man should be found faithful proving himself worthy of trust.

Rewards of the faithful – You have been faithful and trustworthy over a little; I will put you in charge of much.

A workman must be faithful.

Ephesians 1:1: Paul, an apostle (special messenger) of Christ Jesus (the Messiah) by the divine will (the purpose and the choice of God) to the saints (the consecrated, set-apart ones) at Ephesus who are also faithful and loyal and steadfast in Christ Jesus.

Servant

Martyr – one who dies or makes a great sacrifice for a cause.

To serve – work through or perform a term of service., be of use, prove adequate to be of service to, to minister, serving God and serving man also.

Acts 4:27: For in this city there actually met and plotted together against Your Holy Child and Servant Jesus, Whom You consecrated by anointing both Herod and Pontius Pilate, with the Gentiles, and people of Israel were gathered together.

V.29: And now, Lord, observe their threats and grant to Your bond servants (full freedom) to declare Your message fearlessly.

V.30: while You stretch out Your hand to care and to perform signs and wonders through the authority and by the power of the Name of Your Holy Child and Servant Jesus.

Matthew 20:26 -27: Not so shall it be among you, but whoever wishes to be great among you must be your servant. And whoever desire to be first among you must be your slave.

Romans 13:4: For he is God's servant for your good. But if you do wrong (you should dread him and) be afraid for he does not bear and wear the sword for nothing. He is God's servant to execute wrath (punishment, vengeance) on the wrongdoer.

Stewards

D'KONOMOS –Denotes primarily the manager of a household or estate.

Luke 12:42: And the Lord said, "Who then is that faithful <u>steward</u>, the wise man whom his master will set over those in his household service to supply them their allowance of food at the appointed time."

First Corinthians 4:1-2: <u>*Steward* (*trustee*)</u> *of the Word of God.*

First Peter 4:10: As each of you has received a gift (a particular spiritual talent, a gracious divine endowment) employ it for one another as befits good trustees of God's many-sided grace (faithful <u>stewards</u> of the extremely diverse powers and gifts granted to Christians by unmerited favors).

Titus 1:7: For the bishop (an overseer) as God's <u>steward</u> must be blameless, not self-willed, or arrogant or presumptions; he must not be quick- tempered or given to drink or pugnacious (brawling, violent); he must not be grasping and greedy for filthy lucre (financial gain).

First Timothy 4:6: If you lay all these instructions before the brethren, you will be a worthy <u>steward</u> and a good minister of Christ Jesus even nourishing your own self on the truths of the faith and of the good (Christian) instruction which you have closely followed.

First Corinthians 15:58: Therefore, my beloved brethren be firm (steadfast) immovable, always abounding in the work of the Lord (always being superior excelling, doing more than enough in the service of the Lord) knowing and being continually aware that your labor in the Lord is not futile (it is never wasted or to no purpose).

Humble

Humble – To bend the knee, hence, to humiliate

Vanquish – Bring down (low), into subjection, under, <u>humble</u> (self), subdue, to depress, to chasten self, to deal hardly with, defile, exercise, force gentleness, <u>humble</u> (self) submit(self) afflicted.

Numbers 12:3: Now the man Moses was very meek (gentle, kind, and <u>humble</u>) or above all the men on the face of the earth.

Numbers 30:13: Every vow and every binding oath to <u>humble</u> or afflict herself, her husband may establish it, or her husband may annul it.

Deuteronomy 8:2-3a: *And you shall (earnestly) remember all the way which the Lord your God led you these forty years in the wilderness, to <u>humble</u> you and to prove you to know what was in your (mind and) heart, whether you would keep His commandments or not. And He <u>humbled</u> you and allowed you to hunger and fed you with manna, which you did not know nor did your father know.* (**Deuteronomy 8:16; Deuteronomy 21:14; Second Samuel 6:22, and 22:19**)

Second Chronicles 7:14: If my people, who are called by my name, shall <u>humble</u> themselves, pray, seek, crave, and require of necessity My Face and turn from their wicked ways, then will I hear from heaven, forgive their sin and heal their land.

Second Chronicles 12:6; 12:32-36; 33:12,23; 34:27; 36:12

Ezra 8:31   **Job 22:29**   **Psalms 9:12; !0:12,17**
Psalms 68:10; 147:6 **Matthew 5:3; 11:29; 18:4**
Luke 14:11; 18:14   **Romans 12:16**   **Second Corinthians 12:21**
Philippians 2:8;   **James 1:9,10,21** **James 4:10**

First Peter 5:5

First Peter 5:6: Therefore, <u>humble</u> yourselves (demote, lower yourselves in your own estimation) under the mighty hand of God, that in due time He may exalt you.

Submit

Hebrew 13:17: Obey your spiritual leaders and <u>submit</u> to them (continually recognizing their authority over you) for they are constantly keeping watch over your souls and guarding your spiritual welfare, as men who will have to render an account (of their trust). (Do your part to) let them do this will gladness and not with sighing and groaning, for that would not be profitable to you (either).

<u>Submit</u> – To retire withdraw (to <u>yield</u>) give or offer to receive the vision of another and decide to give your life to helping them bring it to fruition or success.

Psalm 18:44   **Psalm 66:3**   **Romans 8:7**
Romans 10:3

Ephesians 5:22: *Wives <u>submit</u> yourselves.*

Hebrew 12:9: Moreover, we have had earthly fathers who disciplined us, and we <u>yielded</u> (to them) and respected (them for training us) Shall we not much more cheerfully <u>submit</u> to the Father of Spirits and so (truly) live.

Hebrew 12:11: For the time being no discipline brings joy, but seems grievous and painful; but afterwards it <u>yields</u> a peaceful fruit of righteousness to those who have been trained by it (a harvest of fruit which consists in righteousness in conformity to God's will in purpose, thought and action, resulting in right living and right standing with God).

James 4:7: <u>*Submit yourself, therefore to God.*</u>

The Spiritual Law of Faith

The deep desire to please God. Obedience to the Word of God. Allegiance to agree with to believe and trust in God, confidence in. Loyalty, to assert without seeing to expect.

Hebrew 11:1: Now! Now! Now! <u>Faith</u> is assurance (confirmation, the title deed) of things <u>hoped</u> for, the proof of things not seen and the conviction of their reality. (faith perceiving as real fact what is not revealed to the senses).

Hebrew 11:2: For by <u>faith</u> – trust and holy fervor born of <u>faith</u>). The men of old had divine testimony borne to them and obtained a good report.

Hebrew 11:3: By <u>faith</u> we understand that the worlds (during the successive ages) were framed (fashioned, put in order, and equipped frothier intended purpose) by the word of God, so that what we see was not made out of things which are visible.

<u>Faith</u> is a law in the Word of God – the Spiritual Law

Romans 10:17: *Faith come by hearing and hearing by the Word of God.*

<u>Faith</u> is acting on; <u>Faith</u> is always an action word. Believing and saying = acting = <u>faith</u>

Mark 11:22: And Jesus replying, said to them have <u>faith</u> in God

(constantly). "Have the God kind <u>faith</u>". The <u>ACTIVATOR – LOVE IS THE MOTIVATOR</u>.

Mark 11:23: Truly I tell you, whoever says to this mountain. Be lifted up and thrown into the sea! And does not <u>doubt at all in his heart but believes</u> <u>that what he says will take place, it will be done for him.</u>

V.24: For this reason, I am telling you, whatever you ask for in prayer, – believe (trust and be confident) that it is granted to you, and you will (get it)!

Mark 2:5	**Luke 5:20**	**Luke 7:9**
Luke 7:50	**Luke 8:48**	**Luke 17:6**
Luke 17:19	**Luke 18:42**	**Luke 22:32**
Acts 11:24	**Acts 3:16**	**Acts 6:5**
Acts 14:9	**Romans 1:8**	**Romans 3:26**
Romans 4:12	**First Corinthians 2:5**	**Romans 10:8**
First Corinthians 12:9	**First Corinthians 13:13**	**Hebrew 6:1**
First Corinthians 16:13	**Second Corinthians 1:24**	**Hebrew 10:22**
Second Corinthians 5:7	**Second Corinthians 10:15**	**Hebrew 11:1**
Hebrew 11:6	**Revelations 2:13**	**Revelation 2:19**
Revelation 13:10	**Revelation 14:12**	**Romans 1:17**
First Timothy 6:12	**First John 5:6**	**James 1:1**

And many, many more examples of scriptures of believing and acting on the Word of God. **Speak it.**

First Corinthians 15:57: *My <u>faith</u> that overcomes the world is my victory.* I am more than a conqueror. **I am a winner.**

Tribute

Tribute – Payment to acknowledge submission, (2) tax, (3) gift or act showing respect.

Genesis 49:15: <u>And he saw that rest was good and that the land was pleasant; and he bowed his shoulders to bear (his burdens) and became a</u> <u>servant to tribute (subjected to forced labor).</u>

Matthew 17:24: When they arrived in Capernaum, the collector of the half- shekel (the temple tax) went up to Peter and said, "Does not your teacher pay the half-shekel?"

Numbers 31:28-29: And levy a <u>tribute</u> to the Lord from the warriors who went to battle, one out of every 500 of the persons, the oxen, the donkey, and the flocks. Take (this <u>tribute</u>) from the warriors; half and give it to Eleazar, the priest as an offering to the Lord.

Numbers 31:28-54

Matthew 22:17-18: Tell us then what You think about this: Is it lawful to pay <u>tribute</u> (levied on individuals and to be paid yearly) to Caesar or not? But Jesus aware of their malicious plot, asked, Why do you put me to the test and try to entrap Me, You pretender (hypocrites)?

V.19: <u>Show me the money</u> used for the <u>tribute</u>, And they brought Him a denarius.

V.20: And Jesus said to them. Whose likeness and title are these?

V.21: They said, Caesar. Then He said to them. Pay therefore to Caesar the things that are due to Caesar and pay to God the things that are due to God. (**Psalm 68:30**)

Royalty

Persons with <u>royal</u> blood, related to a King belonging to a King and to His Kingdom, pertaining to the crown, noble, princely generous receiving support from the King. **The Supreme Ruler.**

Revelations 1:8: I am the Alpha and the Omega, the Beginning, and the End, says the Lord God. He Who is and Who was and Who is to come, the Almighty (the Ruler of all).

Revelations 1:4: John to the seven assemblies (churches) that are in Asia, May grace (God's unmerited favor) be granted to you and spiritual peace (the peace of Christ Kingdom) from Him Who is and Who was and Who is to come, and from the seven Spirits (the sevenfold Holy Spirit) before His throne.

V.5–6: Prince (Ruler) of the kings of the earth. And formed us into a kingdom (a royal race), priest to His God and Father.

Hebrew 8:1: Now the main point of what we have to say is this: We have such a High Priest, One who is seated at the right hand of the Majestic (God) in heaven. (**Psalm 110:1**)

V.2: As officiating priest, a minister in the holy places and in the true tabernacle which is erected not by man but by the Lord.

Hosanna, Hosanna

Hosanna to Our King (Hymn)

Please save us now
Please save us now
Worthy is the Lamb
Praise Glory and Honour Adoration and Love

Man and Angels sing
Glory to our Heavenly King
Hosanna, Hosanna
Please save us now!

Worthy is the Lamb

Precious is our Lord
Glory to the Name
Jesus Christ is Lord
Jesus Christ – Our King
Please save us now!

Blessed be His name
Please save us now
Worthy is our King
Praise be to Him
Hosanna, Please save us now!

Our soon coming King
Jesus Christ in Glory
Holy, Holy, Holy
Hosanna – to our King
Please save us now!
Hosanna to our King.

God Loveth Me

Sometimes I get to thinking of the way You care for me,
And I feel so very humble, that such a thing could be,
For I'm only just a creature, that You fashioned out of clay,
But You're always making sure that I have all I need each day.

Sometimes when I am worried, and I don't know what to do,
And things don't seem to work out, I always run to You.
And what I thought were problems, Vanish 'neath Your hand,
You take the time to listen, and You always understand,

My dwelling may be humble, but You share my small abode,
And when I feel I'm sinking You are there to lift the load,
And I count myself most blessed, as anyone can be,
Because I know beyond a doubt, My Savior loveth me

Author Unknown

In the Secret Place

In the Secret Place of the Most High God, that's where I am,
Where You are is where I want to be.
In His Secret Place, at the Throne of Grace
In the Secret Place of the Most High God, that's where I am.

Out of danger and despair, into peace and where there's no care
I am in Your Holy Place at Your Throne of Grace
In the Secret Place of the Most High God, that's where I am.

I shall not be afraid of the terror of the night,
Nor of the evil that flies in the day, because I trust in Him and …
I am in the Secret Place of the Most High God.

I am in the Secret Place, I am in the Secret Place
In the Secret Place - at the Throne of Grace, that's where I am

His presence surrounding my face, In His Secret Place
In the Secret Place of the Most High God, that's where I am
Stay in the Secret Place long enough to receive your strategy for the
Battle.

The Messianic King According to John's Gospel

Jesus Christ – My Savior (the Anointed One)

John 10:14: *Good Shepherd – I am the Good Shepherd*

John 10:11: And Know my sheep and am known of mine

John 10:16: And they will listen to My Voice and heed My call, and so there will be (they will become) one flock under one Shepherd. (Ezekiel 34:23).

John 10:9: *The Door*

John10:2: But he that entereth in by the <u>door</u> is the Shepherd of the sheep

John 10:7: Then said Jesus unto them again. Verily, Verily, I say unto you, I am the <u>door</u> of the sheep

John 10:9: I am the <u>door</u>, by me if anymore enter in, he shall be saved, and shall go in and out, and find pasture (food).

John 10:10: That thief cometh not but for to steal and to kill and to destroy: <u>I am come that</u> they might have <u>life</u>, and that they might have it more abundantly (in fullest measure) Life-giver.

Resurrection – **John 11:25**

Life - **John 11:25-26, 14:6**

Light – **John 1:7,9**

John 10:16   **John 10:27-30**

Titles of Jesus
(The Messianic King According to John's Gospel)

Word of God

John 1:14: And the Word was made flesh and dwell among us and we beheld His Glory, the (glory as of the only begotten of the Father full of grace and truth.

John 1:14:   Glory

John 1:17: Grace and Truth **John 1:29,36:** Lamb of God **John 1:38:** Rabbi, Master **John 1:41:** Messiah, the Christ

John 1:49: The Son of God, The King of Israel (**John 1:34; John 5:25; 9:35; 10:36**)

John 1:51: The Son of Man (**John 8:28; 12:23; 13:21**) **John 3:16,18:** The only Begotten Son

John 4: 42: The Savior of the World

John 6:33: The Bread of God **John 6:35,48:** The bread of Life **John 6:51:** The Living Bread **John 7:38:** The living Water

Titles of Jesus the Messiah (the Messianic King)

Light of the World – **John 8:12; John 9:5; 11:9**

The King of Righteousness – **Hebrew 7:2**

Thy King Cometh – **John 12:15**

The King of Salem – **Hebrew 7:2**

I am the Way, the Truth, and the Life – **John 1:6**

King of Peace – **Hebrew 7:2** The Father in Me – **John 14:11** I am the True Vine – **John 15:1**

King of the Jews – **John 18:39; 19:3, 19**

Jesus of Nazareth, the King of the Jews – **John 19:19**

Rabboni – Master – **John 20:16**

Jesus is the Christ, the Son of God – **John 20:31**

Lord – **John 21:7,15–16, 20–21**

The Son Jesus Christ, The True God, and Eternal Life – **First John 5:20**

Jesus is the Son Of God – **First John 5:5**

Lord and Savior Jesus Christ – **Second Peter 3:18**

The Stone – **Daniel 2:34**

The Stone which the builders rejected has become the chief Cornerstone, Jesus Christ our Lord – **Psalm 118:22**

Think!

Theme for thought – Philippians 4:8

How wonderful to be
True How Honest are you?
Am I Just?
Does my heart trust?
Do I think about being Pure?
Am I so sure?
Who is Lovely?
And What have Good Report?
Praise God for being Our Source!
The virtue and the Praise
These are all true,
Think on these things,
For the Word of God is for You.

God does marvelous things

When We Pray

Marvelous things, Marvelous things,
God does marvelous things, marvelous things, when we pray.

In His Word He says, Ask and
It shall be done, it shall be done,
God's Word says ask,
'And it shall be done it shall be done, when we Pray

Jesus is the Door, so
Come to the King, Come to the King
Jesus is the Door and
He does marvelous things, marvelous things, when we pray

Open up your heart, and
Let Jesus come in, let Jesus come in,
Open up you heart and
Let Jesus come in, Let Jesus come in,
When we pray
He does marvelous things, He does marvelous things, when we pray.

Good News of the Kingdom

Essential part: Essence of true <u>knowledge</u> for the believer. <u>Jesus is identified as the Word or Logos.</u>

<u>He is the Essence of God's revelation as He lived in this World</u> (quote form Amp. Bible John's Gospel).

Jesus is the Truth: The Lord is coming Soon!

Essence – Second Peter 1:3: Fundamental nature or quality extract, product or what come as the result of applying certain qualities bestowed upon us through His divine power. These things are required and suited to life and godliness through the (full, personal knowledge of Him Who called us by and to His own glory and excellence (virtue)

Psalm 57:8 -9: Awake, my glory (my inner self); awake, harp and lyre! I will awake right early (I will awaken the dawn)! I will praise and give thanks to You, O' Lord, among the people, I will sing praises to You among the nations.

Romans 5:17: For if because of one man's trespass (lapse, offense) death reigned through that one, much more surely will those who receive (God's) over flowing grace (unmerited favor) and the free gift of righteousness (putting them into right standing with Himself) reign as King in life, through the one-Man Jesus Christ (the Messiah, the Anointed One).

John 1:1-4: In the beginning (before all time) was the Word (Christ), and the Word was with God, and the Word was God Himself. He was present originally with God. All thing were made and came into existence through Him; and without Him was not even one thing made that has come into being. In Him was Life and the Life was the Light of men.

V.12: But to as many as did receive and welcome Him. He gave the authority (power, privilege right) to become the children of God, that is, to those who believe in adhere to trust in and rely on) His name.

Luke 21:31-33: Even so, when you see these things taking place, understand and know that the Kingdom of God is at hand. Truly, I tell you, this generation (those living at that definite period of time) will not perish and pass away until all has taken place. The sky and the earth (that is, the universe, the world) will pass away, but my words will not pass away.

Luke 21:27: And then they will see the Son of Man coming in a cloud with great (transcendent and overwhelming) power and (all His Kingly) glory (majesty and splendor).

Ephesians 5:2: And walk in love (esteeming and delighting in one another) as Christ loved us and gave Himself up for us, a slain offering and sacrifice to God (for you, so that it became) a sweet fragrance. **(Ezekiel 20:41)**

The Seven Qualities to the Entrance into the Kingdom of God

Exercising Your Faith to Develop the Power - Virtue

Second Peter 1:11: For so an entrance shall be ministered unto you abundantly into the everlasting Kingdom of our Lord and Savior Jesus Christ.

Second Peter 1:5: And beside this giving all diligence, add to your faith

1. **Virtue** – Moral excellence, firmness of purpose, modest and decent, Christian energy - dumanis "power", add to virtue or develop

2. **Knowledge** - Intelligence, understanding gained by experience, range of information, to know from observation, to discover, ascertain, determine, A greater participation by the knower in the object known, thus more powerfully influencing him. And in (excising) – or putting into action - (develop) or (grow increase or reach full potential).

3. **Self-control** – Control that one exercise over self and its actions, self-restraint, control imposed over self. Presence of mind, coolness imposed over self. Command of feelings. In putting into action self- control grow into

4. **Steadfastness** – Fixed, firm, fast, constant, or firm in resolution, not fickle or wavering, patience, endurance. And in exercising steadfastness (grow increase, reach full potential).

5. **Godliness** (piety) – To the devout, characterized by a Godward attitude to do what is well pleasing to God. Godliness as embodied in, and communicated through, the truth of the faith concerning Christ; and is growing in your full potential as a worshipper of God. And in developing,

6. **Brotherly Affection** – To be pleased with, enjoy approve, pardon, fraternal affection, brotherly love (kindness) love of the brethren and in (exercising) brotherly affection develops Christian love.

The Surety of Calling and Election

Exercising (putting into action) developing (growing and increasing till full potential) in the qualities to an abundance entrance into the eternal Kingdom.

1. **Christian Love** – Is the fruit of His Spirit in the Christian **Galatians 5:22:** *Christian love has God for the primary object and expresses itself first of all in implicit obedience to His commandments. Christian love is not from feelings, not natural* inclination does not always run this love. It seeks the welfare of all – it is unconditional and works no ill to anyone, love seeks opportunity to do good to all men, and especially towards them that are of the household of faith

   Galatians 6:10: *Agape of God*

   Second Peter 1:8: For as these qualities are yours and increasingly abound in you, they will keep (you) from being idle or unfruitful unto the (full personal knowledge) of our Lord Jesus Christ (the Messiah, the anointed one).

   V.9–11: For whoever lacks these qualities is blind, (spiritually) shortsighted, seeing only what is near to him, and has become oblivious (to the fact) that he was cleansed from his old sins.

Because of this, brethren be all the more solicitous and eager to make sure (to ratify, to strengthen, to make steadfast) your <u>calling</u> and <u>election</u> for if you do this, you will never <u>stumble</u> or <u>fall</u>. Thus, there will be richly and abundantly provided for you entry into the eternal kingdom of our Lord and Savior Jesus Christ.

Essence of Substance of
True Knowledge for the Believer
Gospel of God – the Good News of the Kingdom

Essential part – Jesus is the Truth

Second Peter 1:2-3: May grace (God's favor and peace which is perfect, well-being, all necessary good, all spiritual, prosperity and freedom from fears and agitating, passions, and moral conflicts) be multiplied to you in (the full, personal, precise, and correct) knowledge of God and of Jesus our Lord. For His divine power has bestowed upon us all things that (are requisite and suited) to life and godliness, through the (full, personal) knowledge of Him who called us by and to His own Glory and Excellence (virtue).

V.4: By means of these he has bestowed on us His precious and exceeding great promises, so that through them you may escape (by flight) from the moral decay (rottenness and corruption) that is in the world because of covetousness (lust and greed) and become sharers (partakers) of the divine nature.

V.5: For this very reason, adding your diligence (to the divine promises), employ every effort in <u>exercising your faith</u> to develop <u>virtue</u> (excellence, resolution, Christian energy). And in (exercising) <u>virtue</u> (develop) knowledge (intelligence)....

These virtues must be developed in our lives so we can make our calling and election steadfast. If we do this, we will never stumble or fall. (**Second Peter 1:1-11**)

I, like Peter, wants to stir you up by way of remembrance to remind you about these things, although indeed you know them and are firm in the truth that you now hold (**V. 12-13**)

Prayer, Praise of Holy Spirit

This book of hope, love, faith, and joy for all that you go through here on earth. He said, He would be your Father and Friend, Lover and Savior, Redeemer, and Victor, etc. and all that you must do is believe, receive, and accept Jesus as Lord and Savior. Expect Jesus to come in and make a difference in your life through His Word,

John 1:1: In the beginning (before all time) was the Word (Christ), and the Word was with God, and the Word was God Himself.

John 1:2-4: He was present originally with God. All things were made and came into existence through Him; and without Him was not even one thing made that has come into being. In Him was Life, and the Life was the Light of men.

We begin to really live when we accept Christ Jesus into our lives.

John 1:12: But to as many as did receive and welcome Him. He gave the authority (power, privilege, right) to become the Children of God, that is, to those who believe in (adhere to, trust in, and rely on) His Name.

(Isaiah 56:5)

John 1:13: *Who owe their birth neither to bloods nor to the will of the flesh (that of physical impulse) nor to the will of man (that of a natural father) but to God, (They are born of God!)* You can be born again by the will of God! You belong to Him!

John 1:49-51: Nathaniel answered, Teacher, You are the Son of God! <u>You are the King of Israel!</u> Jesus replied, Because, I said to you I saw you beneath the fig tree, do you believe in and rely on and trust in Me? You shall see greater things than this! Then He said to him, I assure you, most solemnly I tell you all, you shall see heaven opened, and the angels of God ascending and descending upon the Son of Man.

Genesis 28:12-14: An he (Jacob) dreamed that there was a ladder set up on the earth, and the top of it reached to heaven' and the Angels of God were ascending and descending on it. And behold, the Lord stood over and beside him and said, I am the Lord, the God of Abraham your father (forefathers) and the God of Isaac, I will give to you and to your descendants the land on which you are lying And your offspring shall be as (countless as) the dust or sand of the ground, and you shall spread abroad to the west and the east and the north and the south; and by you and your offspring shall all the families of the earth be blessed and bless themselves.

Galatians 3:8: And the scripture foreseeing that God would justify (declare righteous, put in right-standing with Himself) the Gentiles in consequence of faith, proclaimed the Gospel(foretelling the glad tidings of a Savior long beforehand) to Abraham in the promise, saying, in you shall all the nations of the earth) be blessed (**Genesis 12:3**)

Galatians 3:29: And if you belong to Christ (are in Him who is Abraham 's Seed) then you are Abraham offspring and (spiritual) heirs according to promise.

Galatians 5:5-6: For we, (not reliving on the Law but) through the (Holy) Spirit's (help) of <u>faith</u> anticipate and wait for the blessing and good or which our righteousness and right-standing with God (our conformity) to His will in purpose, though and actions causes to) to hope. For (if we are) in Christ Jesus, neither circumcision nor uncircumcision counts for anything, but only <u>faith</u> activated, and energized sand expressed and working through <u>love</u>.

The Angel of the Lord (Jesus Christ the King of Glory) called to Abraham from heaven. And said: In blessing, I will bless you and in multiplying I will multiply your descendants like the stars of the heavens and like the sand of the seashore. And your seed (heir) will possess the gate of His enemies.

Psalm 38:15: For in You, O' Lord, do I hope; You will answer, O' Lord my God. For I pray, let them not rejoiced over me, who when my foot slips, they boast against me.

James 1:27: The only religion that God our Father say is as pure and faultless is this, to look after orphans and widows in their distress and to keep oneself from being polluted by the world.

Psalm 147:11: The Lord takes pleasure in those who reverently and worshipfully fear Him, in those who <u>hope</u> in His mercy and loving-kindness.

Psalm 33:18: Behold, the Lord's eye is upon those who fear him (who revere and worship him with alive), who wait for Him and <u>hope</u> in His mercy and loving-kindness.

Proverbs 13:12: <u>Hope</u> deferred makes the heart sick, but when the desire is fulfilled, it is a tree of life.

Lamentations 3:24-26: The Lord is my portion or share, says my living being (my inner self); therefore, will I <u>hope</u> in Him and wait expectantly for Him. The Lord is good to those who wait hopefully and expectantly for Him to those who seek Him (inquire of and for Him and require Him by right of necessity and on the authority of God's word). It is good that one should <u>hope</u> in and wait quietly for the salvation (the safety and ease) of the Lord.

Romans 12:12: Rejoice and exult in <u>hope;</u> he steadfast and patient in suffering; and tribulation; be constant in prayer.

Romans 15:4: For whatever was thus written in former days was written for our instruction that by (our steadfast and patient) endurance and the encouragement (drawn) from the scripture we might hold fast to and cherish <u>hope.</u>

Romans 15:13: May the God of your <u>hope</u> so fill you with all <u>joy</u> and <u>peace</u> in believing (through the experience of your faith) that by the power of the Holy Spirit you may abound and be overflowing (bubbling over) with <u>hope.</u>

First Corinthians 13:13: And so, faith, <u>hope</u>, love, abide (faith) – conviction and belief respecting man's relation to God and divine things; <u>hope</u> – joyful and confident expectation of eternal salvation: love – true affection for God and man, growing out of God's love, for and in us). These three; but the greatest of these is love.

First Corinthians 15:51   **First Peter 1:13**

Ephesians 1:18

Prayer, Praise and Power in God's Kingdom

Hope – Desire with expectation of fulfillment joyful and confident expectation of eternal salvation, look forward, to consider probable or one's due to expect.

First Peter 3:15: But in your hearts set Christ apart as holy (and acknowledge Him) as Lord. Always be ready to give a logical defense to anyone who asks you to account for the <u>hope</u> that is in you, but do it courteously and respectfully.

Isaiah 8:13: Regard the Lord of hosts as holy and honor His Holy Name by regarding Him as your only <u>hope</u>

First Thessalonians 2:19-20: For what is our <u>hope</u> or happiness or our victor's wreath of exultant triumph when we stand in the presence of our Lord Jesus at His coming? Is it not you? For you are (indeed) our glory and our joy!

First Timothy 4:10: With a view to this we toil and strive (yes and) suffer reproach, because we have (fixed our) <u>hope</u> on the living God. Who is the Savior (Preserver, Maintainer, Deliver) of all men, especially of those who believe (trust in, rely on and adhere to Him).

First Timothy 5:4: Now (a women) who is a real widow and is left entirely alone and desolate has fixed her <u>hope</u> on God and perseveres in supplication and prayer night and day.

Ephesians 1:17-18: (For I always pray to) the God of or Lord Jesus Christ, the Father of Glory, that He may grant you a spirit of wisdom and revelation (of insight into mysteries and secrets) in the (deep and intimate) knowledge of Him. By having the eyes of your heart flooded with light, so that you can know and understand the hope to which He has called you and how rich is His glorious inheritance in the saints (His set apart ones).

I am writing this book of hope, love, peace, faith, and joy in the Life of Jesus Christ (the Messiah) to encourage you.

First Peter 1:2 - 3: Who were chosen and foreknown by God the Father and consecrated (sanctified, made holy) by the Spirit to be obedient to Jesus Christ (Messiah) and to be sprinkled, with (His) blood. May grace (spiritual blessing) and peace be given you in increasing abundance (that spiritual peace to be realized in and through Christ's freedom from fears, agitating passions, and moral conflicts). Praised (honored, blessed) be the God and Father of our Lord Jesus Christ (the Messiah)! By His boundless, mercy we have been born again to an ever-living hope, through the resurrection of Jesus Christ from the dead. (**First Peter 1:4-13**)

Prayer, Praise and Practice

Hebrews 11:1: Now faith or (belief and trust, acting on the Word) is the essential part or wealth (pouring forth liberally) of things <u>hoped</u> (desired with, expectation of fulfillment), the evidence (proof or testimony) of things not seen (with the natural eyes but with the spirit or inner vision) dreams or in the imaginations being on the inside.

<u>Prayer:</u> To entreat or request, implore, to call upon, or ask for earnestly, beseech, supplicate to seek by earnest prayer, to petition, to humbly submit to God in prayer, to intercede or stand in the gap for another person or persons. Supplication – earnest prayer, pleas, petition, entreaty, to become one with God united in what God has purposed for you – prayer.

<u>Praise:</u> To celebrate, to bless, to thank, to sing or play music in adoration, to revere and worship, to adore, laudation, hymn, thanks offering, to glorify, applaud, to boast about, to elevate the divinity.

<u>Practice:</u> Perform repeatedly to become proficient, do or perform customarily, habit, exercise for proficiency.

<u>Preach:</u>– Advocate earnestly, announce (good news), to call out, to proclaim, to herald thoroughly, to talk, to announce glad news in advance, to proclaim in advance, report, to make known, reveal, to declare, to tell.

Ephesians 1:17: (For I always pray to) the God of our Lord Jesus Christ, the Father of Glory, that He may grant you a spirit of wisdom and revelation (of insight into mysteries and secrets) in the (deep and intimate) knowledge of Him.

Seek

Beseech – Is from the word "Seek" with the prefix -Be- To go in search, or quest of; to look for; to search for; to take pains to find; often followed, by out; to ask for; to solicit; to try; gain; to resort to, to have recourse to; to aim at; to attempt; to strive after, to inquire of; to endeavor; to make an effort; to pursue; to find or take; to want.

Exodus 33:7   **Job 5:8**   **Deuteronomy 4:29**

First Chronicles 15:13   **Psalm 119:2**   **Psalm 9:10**

First Chronicles 28:9   **Proverbs 8:17**

Isaiah 26:9: ...my spirit within me seeks You... **Matthew 6:33:** Seek (aim at and strive after) **Psalm 2:7:** Seek (unseen but sure) glory **Colossians 3:1:** The higher things.

Psalm 24:6: This is the generation (description) of those who seek Him (who inquire of and for Him, and of necessity require Him).

Matthew 13:17: Truly I tell you many prophets and righteous men (men who were upright and in right standing with God) yearned to see what you see and did not see it, and to hear what you hear and did not hear it.

Matthew 13:19: While anyone is hearing the Word of the Kingdom and not grasp and comprehend it, the evil one comes and snatches away what was sown in his heart. This is what was sown along the roadside.

Second Chronicles 31:21: And every work that he began in the service of the House of God, in keeping with the law and the commandments to <u>seek</u> his God (inquiring of and yearning for Him), he did with all his heart, and he prospered.

The Kingdom of God

Matthew 16:26: For what will it profit a man if he gain the whole world and forfeits his life (his blessed life in the Kingdom of God)? Or what would a man give as an exchange for his (blessed) life in the Kingdom of God?

V.27: For the Son of Man is going to come in the glory (majesty, splendor) of His father with His angels and then He will render account and reward every man in accordance with what he has done.

V.28: Truly, I (Jesus) tell you there are some standing here who will not taste death before they see the Son of Man coming in (into) His Kingdom.

Matthew 19: 28: Jesus said to them, truly I say to you, in the New Age (the Messianic rebirth of the world), when the Son of Man shall sit down on the Throne of His Glory, you who have (become My disciples sided with My party and) followed Me will also sit on twelve thrones and judge the twelve tribes of Israel.

V.29: And <u>anyone</u> and <u>everyone</u> who has left house or brothers or sisters or father or mother or children or lands for my name's sake will receive many (even a hundred) times more and will inherit eternal life.

V.30: But many who (now) are first will be last (then) and many who (now) are last will be first (then).

Matthew 25:31: When the Son of Man comes in His Glory (His Majesty and Splendor) and all the holy angels with Him then He will sit on the Throne of His Glory.

V.32: All nations will be gathered before Him, and He will separate them (the people) from one another as a shepherd separate his sheep from the goats.

V.33: And He will cause the sheep to stand at His right Hand, but the goats at His left.

V.34: Then the King will say to those at the right hand, come, you blessed of My Father (you favored of God and appointed to eternal salvation, inherit (receive as your own) the kingdom prepared for you from the foundation of the world.

V.35: For I was hungry, and you gave Me food, I was thirsty, and you gave Me something to drink, I was a stranger and you brought Me together with yourselves and welcomed and entertained and lodged me.

V.36: I was naked, and you clothed Me, I was sick, and you visited Me with help and ministering care. I was in prison, and you came to see Me.

V.37: Then the just and upright will answer Him. Lord when did we see You hungry and gave You food, or thirsty and gave You something to drink?

V.38: And when did we see You a stranger and welcomed and entertained You, or naked and clothed You?

V.39: And when did we see You sick or in prison and came to visit You?

V.40: And the King will reply to them, Truly I tell you, in so far as you did it for one of the least (in the estimation of men) of these My Brethren, you did it for Me.

Luke 10:28: And Jesus said to him; You have answered correctly; do this and you will live - enjoy active, blessed, endless life in the Kingdom of God.

Matthew 13:43: Then will the righteous (those who are upright and in right-standing with God) shine forth like sun in the kingdom of their

Father. Let him who has ears (to hear) be listening and let him consider and perceive and understand by hearing.

Daniel 12:3: And the teachers and those who are wise shall shine like the brightness of the firmament, and those who turn many to righteousness (to uprightness and right-standing with God) (shall give forth light) like the stars forever and ever.

Daniel 11:32b: But the people who know their God shall prove themselves strong and shall stand firm and do exploits (for God).

The King and His Kingdom

Joel 2:1: Blow the trumpet in Zion, sound an alarm on My Holy Mount (Zion). Let all the inhabitants of the land tremble, for the day of (the judgment of) the Lord is coming, it is close at hand.

Joel 2:11: And the Lord utters His voice before His Army, for His Host is very great and (they are) strong and powerful who execute (God's) Word. For the day of the Lord is great and very terrible, and who can endure it?

Malachi 3:16: Then those who feared the Lord talked often one to another; and the Lord listened and heard it, and a book of remembrance was written before Him of those who reverenced, and worship fully feared the Lord and who thought on His Name.

V.17: And they shall be mine says the Lord of Hosts, in that day when I publicly recognize and openly declare them to be My jewels (My special possession, My peculiar treasure), and I will spare them, as a man spares his own son who serve him.

V.18: Then shall you return and discern between the righteous and the wicked, between him who serves God and him who does not serve Him.

Matthew 25:13: Watch therefore (give strict attention and be cautious and active), for you know neither the day or the hour when the Son of Man will come.

Expectation

Psalms 9:18: For the needy shall not always be forgotten, and the expectation and hope of the meek and the poor shall not perish forever.

Psalms 62:5: My soul wait only upon God and silently submit to Him, for my hope and expectation are from Him.

Proverbs 23:18: For surely there is a latter end (a future and a reward) and your hope and expectations shall not be cut off.

Proverbs 24:14: So, shall you know skillful and Godly Wisdom to be thus to your life; if you find it then shall there be a future and a reward, and your hope and expectation shall not be cut off.

Philippians 1:20a: This is in keeping with my own eager desire and persistent expectation and hope, that I shall not disgrace myself nor be put to shame in anything.

Expectation – To await, hope, intense anticipation to consider probable or one's due, to look forward to, apprehension. Always let expectation be high and trust that what you have believed you have received.

Hebrew 11:10: For he was (waiting expectedly and confidently) looking forward to the city which has fixed and firm foundations, whose Architect and Builder is God.

Jude 1:21: Guard and keep yourselves in the love of God, expect and patiently wait for the mercy of our Lord Jesus Christ (the Messiah) – which will bring you) unto life eternal.

V.22: And refute (so as to) convict some have mercy who waver and doubt.

V.23: (Strive to) save others, snatching (them) out of (the) fire; on others take pity (out) with fear, loathing even the garment spotted by the flesh and polluted by their sensuality.

V.24: Now to Him, Who is able to keep you without stumbling or slipping or falling, and to present (you) unblemished (blameless and faultless) before the presence of His Glory in triumphant, joy, and exultation (with unspeakable, ecstatic delight)

V.25: To the one only God, or Savior through Jesus Christ our Lord, be glory (splendor), majesty, might and dominion and power and authority, before all time and now and forever (unto all the ages of eternity) Amen (So be it).

Revelation 3:20: Behold, I stand at the door and knock; if anyone hears and listens to and heeds My voice and opens the door, I will come into him and will eat with him, and he (will eat) with Me.

V.21: He who overcome (is victorious). I will grant him to sit beside Me on My Throne, as I myself overcame (was victorious) and sat down beside My Father on His throne.

V.22: He who is able to hear, let him listen to and heed what the (Holy) spirit says to the assemblies (churches) Amen!

Revelations 4:1: *After this I looked and behold a door standing open in heaven!*

Printed in the United States
by Baker & Taylor Publisher Services